A Rabbi At Sea

A Uniquely Spiritual Journey

RABBI CORINNE COPNICK

ISBN: 978-1-6847-1495-7 (sc)
ISBN: 978-1-6847-1496-4 (e)

The author is available for speaking and media engagements.
Contact information:
rabbi@rabbicorinne.com
www.rabbicorinne.com

Scripture taken from the *JPS Hebrew-English Tanakh: The Traditional Hebrew Text and the New JPS Translation, 2nd ed.* (Philadelphia: The Jewish Publication Society, 1999-5759).

Back cover photo: ©Aaron Keigher Photography, 2015

Lulu Publishing Services rev. date: 02/13/2020

Lulu Press, Inc.
1663 Liberty Drive,
Suite 200,
Bloomington, IN 47403
1-888-265-2129

What people say about A RABBI AT SEA...

"Sparks of God's light are scattered all over the world. According to the tradition of Jewish mysticism, it is our responsibility to find them, elevate them, and share their glory. Rabbi Copnick's unique ability to perceive these divine sparks is a blessing to us all. The stories of her discoveries are inspiring and breathtaking. She reassures us that God is to be found almost everywhere if only we look with open eyes and a sensitive heart."
—*Rabbi Ed Feinstein, Senior Rabbi, Valley Beth Shalom Synagogue, Los Angeles*

"Rabbi Corinne Copnick has written an extraordinary, artistic testimony to the majestic wonder of nature and the human beings and animals who inhabit it. With her keen, inquisitive eye, open heart, and the sublime story telling of a consummate artist, she brings us on a journey of discovery, and we are left with a unique spiritual experience. Her book touches our MINDS as she illuminates the practices of ancient and contemporary cultures, touches our HEARTS as it takes us to places we never expected to traverse, and reaches our SOULS as it awakens us to the power and grace of our Creator. This unique, creative work will stay with you long after you put it down, and you will be filled with gratitude to Rabbi Copnick's love letter to the gift of being alive in our world."
—*Rabbi Mel Gottlieb, President, Academy for Jewish Religion, California*

"*A Rabbi at Sea* is a marvelous offering, an absolutely charming narrative that teaches as it delights."
—*Rabbi Beth Lieberman, Founder, Lehrhaus Literary*

"Written with a warm, loving, and whimsical touch, Rabbi Corinne's stories give us fresh perspective and inspire us to travel and marvel the world. What an extraordinary woman and a true role model!"

—*Rabbi Belle Michael, Campus Rabbi, Cal Lutheran University; Rabbi, Kehilla Shira Hadasha*

"A person who converts to Judaism recites the *Shema*, the declaration of God's Oneness as part of their immersion in the *Mikveh*, the Jewish ritual bath Rabbi Copnick describes in her story, 'Follow the *Mikveh*.' *A Rabbi at Sea* would make engaging reading for anyone considering conversion to Judaism as it depicts the diversity of Jewish experience and ritual throughout the world and over time, engages us in questions with which people everywhere struggle, and portrays the diverse beauty of the Creator's world."

—*Chaplain Muriel Dance, Ph.D., BCC, Executive Director, Sandra Caplan Community Beit Din, Los Angeles*

"*A Rabbi at Sea* is an empowering story of the very real possibilities that exist for unprecedented inner growth and exciting adventures beyond the biblical three score years and ten. This book is an inspiration for each of us to boldly embrace opportunities to remain fully alive, all the days of our lives."

—*Julie G. Madorsky, M.D.*

Dedicated to my children,
Janet Wendy, Shelley Lynne, Susan Ilene, and Laura Beth,
their partners-in-life, Ira Joel and Ruth Ann,
and my grandchildren,
Joshua Samuel, Samantha Isabel, Rachel Genna,
and the memory of Sienna Rae and Albert.
You are the tender music of my heart.

LULLABY

Here
violin
strings
vibrate
Mosaic
dreams
in percussion.
Color
and
light
resonate
shadows
in freshly
reflecting
waves.
Here
Miriam
who watched
a child
lullabies
the sea.

CONTENTS

SECTION IX   APPENDIX

FOREWORD

*R*abbi Copnick's road to the rabbinate is as unusual as her road since becoming ordained. You will read a bit about the former in the ensuing pages and a good deal about the latter. To give you a taste, while most people are enjoying well-deserved retirement, at age seventy-three, Corinne began her six year course of study and, remarkably, was ordained rabbi at the age of seventy-nine.

Ordination, however, was to be the beginning of a new adventure. Rabbi Copnick (or Rabbi Corinne, as she is known) has had an unconventional "pulpit" and her "congregants," and we readers, are the richer for it. Through these pages, with Rabbi Corinne as our guide, we vicariously tour lands from Australia (where you'll meet the world's smallest species of penguin) to Curacao, Brazil, Dubrovnik ("elegant, with cobblestone roads and graceful buildings that look as if they could be finely-drawn illustrations..."), Panama, Singapore, New Caledonia, Casablanca, Cambodia and many more. Her insights about the culture and the people she encounters are thoughtfully embedded in her accounts.

You'll "experience" the Jewish High Holidays on a cruise ship and likely be touched by the poignant story of the man who blew the *shofar*. And you'll enhance your Jewish education as she explains Jewish customs and laws she incorporates with her seaworthy congregants. Perhaps most of all, you will likely marvel at Rabbi Copnick's enthusiasm for her rabbinate. Pack your imaginary bags, walk the gangway, and enter your stateroom as you cruise the seas and fascinating shores that lie ahead.

Rabbi David Woznica,
Stephen Wise Temple, Los Angeles, California

PREFACE

by Janet Spiegel, Shelley Spiegel, Susan Spiegel, and Laura Spiegel

*J*ANET: When my mom entered her seventies, she was considering going back to graduate school to become a rabbi. At the time, it seemed impossible. Most seminaries required a first year abroad in Israel. Others were too far away to contemplate a daily commute. So, when she learned that AJR-CA (the Academy for Jewish Religion, California) was offering a Master of Rabbinic Studies program, one particularly interested in attracting mature students, my mom gave it serious consideration. Against the odds, at seventy-three, my mother was admitted as a very mature rabbinic student, and at seventy-nine, after six exciting, challenging and full years of study and collegiality, was proud to give her graduation speech on the *bima* (platform) as a full-fledged rabbi.

She had already founded *Beit Kulam*, a community-based study group that was growing in popularity and attracting attention from other Jewish groups, when amazingly, she was invited by a prestigious cruise line to fill their need for an onboard guest rabbi! It was incredible. She was allowed to bring one guest. I was not a cruiser by nature. I was worried about sea sickness and claustrophobia, so, after no real debate at all, my sister Susan went with her on her first THREE cruises. When cruise number FOUR was offered, they both decided that I was going, fears or not…and off I went on a European tour by sea. To my surprise, not only did I love cruising, but seeing the world through my mother's lens was mind-opening. Traveling with my mother is like having your own personal docent. It's strange as an adult to contemplate being in the same stateroom with your parent for twenty, thirty, forty days at a time, and yet, just as the sea has its rhythm, we too, found our stride. My mom and I had always been good travel partners on land. It turns out that we were great travel partners at sea as well.

Our goal on every journey, was to uncover, discover, and dissect Jewish life (hoping we would find it) in every country we visited. It gave us our own mission, in addition to the ship offerings. Often our Jewish discoveries abroad were joyful, as you'll experience in many of the following stories, and others so deeply heartbreaking, particularly when we could find little to no trace of Jewry, where once there had been robust community in decades and centuries past, in so many other countries. Sadly, dogged persecution throughout history has left Jewish life very slim in most parts of the world outside of the US and Israel. Small populations remain, other than France, across most of Europe and very little elsewhere. Overall, though, we felt like Jewish detectives, sussing out little-known bits of information and weaving our own cloth out of the Jewry we could find around the world. But where we could find it, we joyously celebrated the connections we could make.

My mother's stories that follow are heartfelt and deeply insightful. Students of Jewish history and contemporary Jewish global presence will discover a treasure trove of perspective within the following pages. Rabbi Corinne, my mom, takes you along with her (and us) around much of the globe and just as we, her daughters, gained perspective and a fuller understanding of the tapestry of world Jewry as we traveled with her, it is our hope that, as you vicariously travel with us, you'll enjoy her insights and humor, feel embraced by her teachings, learn from her discoveries, and be enveloped by her humanity and global perspective along the way.

* * * *

SHELLEY: If you had told me thirty years ago that my mother would be galivanting around the world on glamorous cruise ships in her eighties, serving as a Rabbi, socializing with and enlightening the minds and souls of travelers, I would have had a good chuckle. However true that may be, I am simply not surprised! My mother, "Rabbi Corinne," is truly a unique and remarkable woman who only grows more interesting and inspirational with each passing year. In fact, just the other day, I shared with my own daughter how incredibly lucky I was—not only to have such an exceptionally talented, gracious, and kind woman as a mother, but also as a role model; to have the opportunity to learn from her, because she is continually growing.

This book is an insightful, first hand observation into the history and condition of Judaism in various locales, through the appreciation of culture, travel, and humanity itself. I especially enjoyed learning more about the beautiful and varied places on our not-so-large earth and feel gratitude and connection, as though I've almost traveled these places myself. It gives me a great sense of satisfaction and happiness to feel as though I was able to travel along with her, through her stories. I hope you enjoy this wonderful work through the insights of Rabbi Corinne Copnick as much as I have!

* * * *

SUSAN: My mother, Rabbi Corinne, once shared with me that we are all a culmination of our experiences. Our experiences make us who we are, so when the opportunity arose to travel to new parts of the globe with her, I enthusiastically embraced the adventure.

Traveling around the world, to far-away places that encompass different cultures, different religions, difference landscapes, different languages, different food, different currency, different fashion, and diversity at every level makes you appreciate—well, most simply put, our differences! And, it was wonderous when these differences, on some occasions, turned out to be more similar than one might believe. I learned a lot about a lot: new people, new places, new things!

I have always felt spiritually connected to the universe, but not particularly religious and relatively agnostic. So—when, during these travels, the Rabbi and I sought out Jewish landmarks at every port, the history of each was rife with stories of atrocities that affected me deeply, and rich with tales of perseverance and pride that inspired me. I have always been proud to be Jewish but now feel more connected—definitely more connected to the Jewish culture found in all of these different places around the world. I am blessed to have a mother who is endlessly creative and beautiful on every level.

* * * *

LAURA: During the course of her life, my mother, Rabbi Corinne, has traveled many tides, and has expertly navigated many voyages— journeys through worlds, through time, and conceptually, through dimensions seen and unseen. Her profound sense of connection to the totality of human experience is inspiring.

A Rabbi at Sea is a light-hearted, refreshing glimpse into the crossover of human interaction and engagement. My mother's stories reflect her welcoming of both sameness and difference in a wide, enriching embrace.

I, along with my partner, Ruth, have been fortunate to engage in weekly Torah portion study with such an opened-minded and gifted soul, consistently curious about all the elements of living. While traveling through Jewish history in this fashion, I sense that our collegial conversations occur amidst divine inspiration.

My mother has given birth to me in so many ways, and for that she holds the honor of being my heroine. How fitting that we four daughters, who represent resounding joy to her in this journey called Life, contribute to this Preface!

A TRAVELER'S PRAYER[1]

Eternal God, Protector of our ancestors,
When You are near, our strength is here.
May it be Your Will to sojourn at our side,
And bless us on this joyful journey
Through air and land and sea,
At peace with your creations
In all their diversity.

Eternal God, may our faith in You,
And the good work of our hands,
Give succor, support, and hope
For health, happiness, and harmony
To those in need everywhere.
And may Your love guide us securely
Home to our families and friends.
Blessed are You, Adonai, Protector of Israel.

TRAVELING TOWARDS A DREAM[2]

Some dream of fortune,
Some dream of fame,
Some dream of things
That could have been.
Stop, rewind,
We'll map our minds,
We're traveling towards a dream.

Some dream of fortune,
Some dream of fame,
Some dream of things
They've never seen.
Stop, recharge,
Our courage large,
We're traveling towards a dream.

SECTION ONE

South Pacific, Oceania

Section 1, Oceania, South Pacific
Native totems intermingle with Catholic grave markers at
moving war memorial on Isle des Pins, New Caledonia.
Photo credit: Susan Spiegel©2015.

Az der Rebbe Geyt – A Rabbi at Sea

Over the past few years since I entered my eighties, I have been contemplating retirement. I seem to have actually "retired" several times from my varied careers, but then, drawn by the attraction of a compelling new interest, I keep on reinventing myself as only "semi-retired." In the process, I have come to believe that a rabbi never completely retires. Maybe that's true for many seniors whose passions lie in other fields. In any case, as a non-retired, retired rabbi, I have served as Guest Staff Rabbi for both Passover and the Jewish High Holy Days on a number, seven to be exact, of delightful, lengthy cruises. It has afforded me the luxury of traveling, accompanied by either Susan or Janet, two of my four daughters, to many fascinating, faraway places in the world that I could never have otherwise visited.

As an American, pluralistic rabbi, it has given me the opportunity to explore Jewish communities in other countries, many of them now only a memory recorded in a small museum or a series of plaques, or a "Jew street" where once its inhabitants conducted commerce. A few communities are small but still vibrant, maintaining customs different from the ones I am used to celebrating at home. Some are still Jewish— despite the inherent difficulties. I have visited countries like Indonesia where Judaism is not one of their six official religions, and where a crew member with an Israeli passport could not disembark. I have also visited Jewish communities that are still substantial and thriving, such as Australia or Brazil. Or countries like Spain which have been offering citizenship to Jews who can show ancestry to relatives expelled or persecuted at the time of the Inquisition (but with a time-limited offer) and, more recently, Portugal (with no time limit); or Morocco, which, in an appealing new spirit of harmony, now welcomes all religions, putting aside the fact that most Moroccan Jews—who had migrated to that country even before the Spanish Inquisition and lived peacefully with the Berbers—were shamefully persecuted and thus forced to flee when Israel declared itself a state. I have visited Rhodes in Greece where a tall, black memorial records the death in the Holocaust of the 1,600 Jews who once lived there. And so on.

So I was taken aback when a more stationary American rabbi asked me a rather startling question the other day: "Do people on cruise ships really want to attend a religious service?" he asked.

"When you're in the middle of the Atlantic Ocean without sight of land—just seemingly endless waves—for a week before reaching a port," I replied, "it certainly puts you in a receptive state of mind to find some time to have a conversation with God."

Actually the passengers on board who identify as Jewish (in my experience, anywhere from twenty-four on a smaller ship to sixty-eight on a mid-size ship) welcome the chance to celebrate a sacred Jewish ritual together as a "community within a community." For me, it is a joyful experience to welcome people who come from different countries, speak various languages and practice diverse traditions, but are still delighted to celebrate on an ocean-going voyage with other Jews.

At one shipboard Passover *Seder* (a ritual feast following a sequential order), for example, I asked for volunteers to read the traditional "Four Questions" with Yiddish, French, Spanish, Ladino, and English translations at hand, symbolic languages of some of the countries in which Jews dispersed from the Holy Land had lived for centuries, if not thousands of years. Then all the "congregants" at the *Seder* tables read them together in Hebrew (transliteration provided).

And although the meal was kosher (I spend a lot of time working out the menu with the always cooperative Director of Food Services and the talented Executive Chef), and the wine chosen was an excellent kosher Baron de Hirsch brand, I knew someone would pipe up with, "I usually have Manischewitz," and of course we did have that traditional square bottle of VERY SWEET wine too.

The tables were gorgeously set with "kept only for Passover" dishes, beautiful scrolled menus, flowers, white tablecloths, place cards, a

Haggadah at each place setting, and wine glasses, of course, which the waiters made sure to fill four times on cue. Ceremonial platters containing the symbols of Passover were on each table of eight. The ship's techies had arranged a microphone for me so that everyone could hear the service and my remarks.

For me, one of the most moving moments occurred before the *Seder* when a non-Jewish couple asked if they could attend. "Our daughter converted and is married to a Jewish man, and our son-in-law invites us to their home every Passover," they explained. "We're far away now, but we'd like to feel close to them."

So they came to the *Seder*—despite the fact that Good Friday coincided with Passover this year, and there was a priest aboard to lead Easter services—and they enjoyed it immensely. As well, we had a Messianic couple (considering conversion to Judaism) also in attendance.

For the second night, I held a discussion group on "Counting the *Omer*" (collected barley sheaves to represent time)," and to my surprise, a considerable group attended. Soon we would begin to stop at ports every day, but people still attended the *Yizkor* (Memorial) service on Friday night, which I coupled with Holocaust remembrance. I invited the priest, my Catholic counterpart aboard, to recite the twenty-third Psalm, which he was delighted to do. He had been a missionary in North Africa for many years and was now the director of his country's missions in various places.

We did have one controversy aboard as to whether Passover should be seven or eight days. We settled on seven days (which is the modern norm in Israel and also for Reform congregations), but if anyone preferred eight days, that was okay too. We still had plenty of *matzah* (ceremonial flatbread) at hand.

Lots of good, often very accomplished people on the ship. And, oh yes, since we had a passenger aboard who was born in Morocco, we had a *Mimouna*, something I had never celebrated before. It's held to mark the end of Passover and features lots and lots of delicious pastries, Moroccan style. In Israel, *Mimouna* (the name honors Maimonides) is marked by a general Open House, and people go from house to house sampling all the desserts.

So the answer to my fellow rabbi's question is: "Yes, it's really possible to conduct religious services on a cruise ship, and many people are happy to come—and, indeed, grateful that these services are provided." Of course, not every cruise line provides this service (unless it's specifically a Jewish-oriented cruise), and in most cases, it's left up to the passengers to conduct their own services if they wish to do so.

And no, my friends, I don't get seasick, and I love being at sea with diverse people from many lands.

It is my hope that *A Rabbi at Sea* will stimulate your own spiritual journey, as these voyages did for me, and I've provided suggestions for discussion, or just to think about, in an Appendix ("Study Guide for Book Clubs") at the end of the story.

When a Lemon Trumps an Etrog: Spiritual Connection in the South Pacific

*I*t was on a middle-sized cruise ship (1,000 to 1,500 passengers plus crew) shortly after I had been ordained that I realized how much I had absorbed from my six years of rabbinic education. Like the medical doctor of an earlier time who made house calls with a medical bag in tow, I had taken a small suitcase of books with me, as well as the short sermons and other material I had pre-prepared in file folders before boarding the ship in Vancouver, Canada for the High Holy Days. Now my daughter, Susan, and I were headed for the South Pacific. I knew that I would have very limited access to the Internet for supplementary material, so I had taken the precaution of bringing a dozen copies of specific services and—since plants or fruit could not be brought onto the ship—of preparing a bubble-wrapped *lulav* with artificial leaves representing the palm, myrtle, and willow bound together for *Sukkot* (a festival of thanksgiving for the autumn harvest) services. These were my materials. The rest was in my head and heart. In addition, as the rabbi on the cruise ship, I would have to adapt to the different rooms and schedules assigned for religious services. They would be empty rooms until I used my then newly-minted rabbinic capabilities to make them into *Makoms*, into sacred spaces, and the diverse people who would come to fill them into a temporary community.

Well into the cruise, a woman with slightly graying hair, Bernadine, hugged me joyfully in the corridor outside the room where I had just conducted an *Erev Shabbat* (evening before the Sabbath) prayer service. Our ship was a mere dot on the vast Pacific ocean at the time, voyaging between Vancouver (Canada) and Sydney (Australia). On the way we had already visited some of the many groups of Pacific islands: Hawaii (Honolulu), American Samoa (a US territory where the indigenous people are intent on preserving their culture, yet there are many churches of various denominations, with the Mormon Church predominating); Fiji (only 133 of 300 plus islands are inhabited); Vanuatu (Mystery Island, an uninhabited island traditionally considered haunted at night); and New Caledonia (formerly a French colony, where American troops were stationed during WWII). But at that moment of Bernadine's hug, all we could see through the ship's many large windows were sky and sea melting into one another. A time and place to marvel at the works of the divine, indeed.

"I have the courage now," Bernadine cried, happy tears escaping down her cheeks. "I thought I was too old, but you inspired me." She had been working with seniors for years and had long yearned for but hesitated to enter a degree program in gerontology. "I'm going to take the plunge," she confided. With his arm around her shoulders, her husband nodded his own encouragement. They were both devout Catholics. We had first met when I was invited to "preach" at one of the Catholic masses held daily on the ship. On another occasion, I was asked to read a passage from the Old Testament. In return, the priest (a retiree) attended most of our Jewish services—where I honored him in a similar fashion.

In a meaningful interfaith service at the Arizona Memorial in Oahu, all the on-board clergy (the Catholic priest, the Protestant minister, and myself as rabbi) participated jointly in memorializing the men who died at sea at Pearl Harbor—the infamous attack that caused the US to declare war on Japan. After that deeply felt occasion, we three clergy enjoyed having several lunches together. We discussed religious similarities and differences among our respective faiths. Their congregational concerns were very much like those we face in Jewish life today: declining membership and attendance; making religion relevant to a new generation; intensified focus on educating youth; attending to the changing needs of a growing elderly population more likely now to stay in their homes than opt for costly assisted-living residences; interference in (or fear of) speaking from the pulpit about public issues that needed to be addressed; and, yes, we talked honestly about Israel.

So did a number of people (both Jews and non-Jews) who would approach me from time to time on the ship to ask challenging questions, things they were too reticent to ask in more formal settings. Some were evangelical Christians who wanted me to know that they were definitely "pro-Israel." One person asked me if sacrifices still figure in Judaism today, and if the blood libel had any truth to it. Another man quoted chapter and verse from the Book of Daniel and wanted to know why, in the light of these prophecies, Jews still would not accept Jesus as their Messiah. Fortunately, my pluralistic rabbinic training had prepared me to field questions such as these. I always had to be "on" as a rabbi.

My tour of duty also included *Sh'mini Atzeret* on the eighth day of *Sukkot* (it was fun to pray for rain with water, water all around us!) and a joyful *Simchat Torah* (renewal of the Torah reading cycle). Our little Jewish "community" all took turns reading from Rabbi Plaut's *Torah: A Modern Commentary* (since we didn't have a Torah scroll) mainly in English. Other than an Israeli couple (and an American who lived half the year in Eilat) who made up my regular *minyan* of some twenty people—a good turnout considering the small proportion of Jews on the ship—none of my "congregants" could read Hebrew.

There were always wonderful surprises, however. At one Passover *Seder*, a group of thirteen Israelis traveling together read the list of the plagues visited on Egypt and related prayers in Hebrew with such melodic gusto that when we all got to sing *Dayenu* (it is enough), the words of the traditional song seemed well suited to the occasion.

On another cruise, I had prepared for Purim (the holiday where participants shake noisemakers and boo the villain, Haman, who tried to get the Jews of Shushan killed long ago) by making a portable Festival scroll that I could roll up and take on the ship. One by one, I printed out the many pages of the *Megillah* (Book of Esther) on thick, quality paper from a computer program providing both the Hebrew text and the musical notation marks called "tropes" above the page. Then I pasted the many attractive pages together, page by page, to form a scroll that told the story of the holiday. I tied it up with a pretty ribbon and put in my suitcase. It was a successful combination of woman and machine.

The Festival tropes for Purim (the way you sing the Hebrew text is called "cantillation") are different from the way the text is sung on

7

other occasions. Lo and behold, we had not one, but two members of our little congregation who knew the Purim tropes (but had never before met one another) and could not only read the scroll but also sing it. This is no mean feat.

"I studied these tropes for my *Bar Mitzvah*," said the man, a Montrealer, whose Judaic coming of age ritual had taken place at least forty years previously. He still remembered every word and its melody.

The second participant, a woman living in New York but originally from Israel, was equally well-versed in both the text and the music. Together, as we unrolled the scroll, stretching it between the two of them—it reached across the room—these volunteer readers took turns cantillating the text. A third person helped in holding up the scroll for the two readers. It was, indeed, the whole *Megillah* (a very long story).

Our congregants were with our readers all the way, absolutely amazed that this was actually happening. At the conclusion of the reading, they all clapped and cheered and stamped their feet, and made lots of happy noise. It was a joyful Purim indeed! We were all very much alive.

It was so satisfying to shape such disparate people—from Canada, Australia, England, America, Mexico, and Israel—into a little community that gleefully took the two loaves of *challah* and two bottles of ritual wine the ship provided for us for the festivals and Sabbath eves into the dining room for Friday night dinner together. They even approached several "Jews who don't go" and encouraged them to join our Friday night services.

One couple who live in Mexico asked if I would be willing to travel there to lead services in their small, artistic community's synagogue. Their lay rabbi had left for a bigger synagogue in another town. "We can't pay you," she said, "but you'd have a nice vacation and a place to stay. We could probably pay your airfare." A very nice offer, but unfortunately, I still have to pay back my student loans.

However, my experiences as Guest Staff Rabbi (this was only my second cruise; I've since had five more) can't be measured in dollars and cents. Being a cruise rabbi demands adjustment to the personalities and prayer expectations of people who may be from Reform, Conservative, Modern Orthodox, and even alternative backgrounds. In my conversations with some Israelis on the ship, they defined themselves as secular Jews, yet they consider the Orthodox way the only "right" way to be Jews.

That's why Lenny—who "goes to *shul* only once a year and that's enough!"—couldn't bring himself to accept an artificial *lulav*, electric candles (because we were not allowed to light real ones on the ship), and a lemon from the ship's kitchen instead of an *etrog* (the fourth species, a member of the citrus family) for *Sukkot*, the Jewish harvest celebration in the autumn. "A lemon is not an *etrog*," he said excitedly. He is right. It's not. But where do you get a fresh *etrog* in the middle of the South Pacific ocean on a twenty-five-day cruise? At least we had dinner together in a temporary shelter (okay, not a branch-covered hut, but at least an Ark of sorts). On the first night of *Sukkot*, we waved the artificial *lulav* in every direction (which way was east?), thanked God that we had survived to this season, and invited imaginary guests to join us. When we stepped outside on deck, looked at the stars, and inhaled the cresting waves, we were a community, joyful and hopeful for the future.

Later, when we explored *Isle des Pins* (Island of Pines), one of the New Caledonian islands, we climbed about 150 rough-hewn, slippery stone steps to reach a tiny church that was several hundred years old and still in use. Originally built by Catholic missionaries using indigenous artisans who put into play their imaginative woodcarving, it was perched high on a mountain top. At the rear of the church, overlooking the sea, stood a tall Catholic memorial carved in stone. At its top, a saintly stone figure held a cross aloft, Statue of Liberty style. The memorial was dedicated to the men of the island who had served France in two World Wars. And circling the memorial stone were native totems, tall ones to recognize those who had been high chiefs, as was the native custom. In between the tall totems were symmetrically interspersed, shorter totems to signify lower orders in the indigenous hierarchy. Here, in this beautiful, natural setting with abundant flowers, traditional Catholicism was mixed with native culture—a phenomenon we call "syncretism" today—to honor the men who had given their lives for freedom.

One might say, comparatively speaking, that this memorial was not exactly an oval-shaped, bumpy-skinned *etrog* in its adherence to strict religious belief, but in its combined purpose of respect paid and beauty intended to elevate and comfort, it was like a fresh lemon, golden yellow and round. It was both touching and reverent. As this blended memorial etched itself into the camera of my memory, it supported my belief as a "new" rabbi that the spirit of religion often supersedes the letter of the law.

Money Speaks Freedom in New Caledonia–in French!

*N*ew Caledonia, a French-speaking collectivity of our South Pacific stop-over islands on the way to Australia—about 750 miles away—definitely has a *je ne sais quoi*, an indefinable special quality. The New Caledonian islands consist of *Grande Terre*, the Loyalty islands, the Chesterfield islands, the Belearchipelago, the aforementioned *Isle des Pins*, and a few remote islets. I loved *Isle des Pins* when we stopped there—oh, the nostalgic smell of pine trees for someone born in Canada! These islands attract birdwatchers from around the world.

This group of islands was very different from other South Pacific Islands I visited, however. For one thing, it's noticeable that tropical flora does not have a monopoly on the landscape; trees and plants that are more familiar to the Northern Hemisphere mingle with more exotic varieties here. The temperature, too, seemed more moderate when we visited the capital, Noumea, on *Grande Terre*.

The residents of *Grande Terre* pride themselves on being a little Paris of the South Pacific. Most people we encountered could speak English, but the preferred language of this island today is French. The shop windows are fashion savvy and show a high degree of sophistication in the expensive, quality products they display. There are excellent museums, especially the ones that review the World Wars, both I and II. Even the money is French (ah, but New Caledonian French), as we soon discovered when we tried to exchange US dollars for New Caledonian francs (surprisingly, they were worth more than American dollars) at the island's main bank.

You see, the island's policy is not to accept any foreign money at all, not even US dollars. All visitors must change the money of their country of origin to New Caledonian dollars. And if you don't spend it all, you can't exchange what is left for your own currency. Since my daughter and I did not have much time to spend on the island, we calculated that exchanging $20.00 US would be ample. We thought that touring the much touted (deservedly) World War II museum would take a couple of hours. That, and a cup of coffee, would consume the time at our disposal before we had to return to the ship.

But we could not exchange the $20.00 US. No way, no how. Not at the bank machine, not in the bank. The minimum amount exchangeable was $50.00 US. The museum's admission price was the equivalent of $2.00 US, so for the two of us, that made $4.00 US. Certainly enough money would remain for a delectable shared French pastry at the corner café and possibly an espresso. *Non, non, non.* Not possible. It was $50.00 US or nothing.

Americans from the US are not used to discovering that there are corners of the world where their money is scorned. But rejected our dollar bills were. That was the pleasantly-stated decree of the three elegantly dressed beauties—coiffed, made up, bejeweled—as they sat on the stools that graced the long front-counter of the bank. The cashier proffered the same opinion from her caged window at the back of the bank, and, despite our pleas, the even more beautiful and fashionable manager finally summoned from her secluded office confirmed what her employees had said. Nothing less than $50.00 US could be exchanged into New Caledonian money. And no remnant of that money could be changed back.

Until…

Noting that the gorgeous manager's English was tinged with a French accent—not any old French but quite obviously Parisian French, we began to converse with her in French. New Caledonia reminded us so much of France, we enthused, even of Paris. Oh, yes, we had visited Paris, and, *mais oui*, of course we spoke French because we were born in Montreal. A French city. So much in common. Suddenly, she was willing to make a one-time exception. The bank *would* exchange twenty American dollars for us. We exchanged smiles and little pleasantries along with the money. In well-tutored French all around.

New Caledonian money in hand, there was still time for us to enjoy the World War II museum. It is truly a wonderful museum. With considerable artistry and modern technology, it depicts, not only the course of this war as experienced in New Caledonia, but also how such a diverse community, made up of so many different nationalities and ethnic groups, especially the aboriginals, were knit together by war. The population of these islands is a mix of the *Kanakas* (the original inhabitants), people of European ancestry, Polynesians, Southeast Asians, and those few descended from the *Pied-Norand Maghrebans*. Periods of slavery ("blackbirding") were also part of their history. The two hours my daughter and I spent at the museum were not enough to completely absorb all this information.

However, the museum exhibition did help us understand how, for years and years, the island had been batted back and forth between so many foreign empires, and why it was so important for the islanders to maintain their independence from foreign influence. These deeply-entrenched feelings extend to their money. Their economy is strong—they have some of the largest deposits of nickel in the world, which gives these islands prosperity and financial independence. New Caledonia will therefore conduct its affairs in NEW CALEDONIAN money.

After our museum visit, there was insufficient time for a French pastry or *café-au-lait* before returning to our ship. But we had gained a valuable understanding. The left-over New Caledonian dollars that remained in our wallets now had a special significance: New Caledonia was no longer a colony of any foreign power. Its non-exchangeable dollars stood for freedom—and unity.

A Ping in the Middle of the Ocean

W hen I moved in 1985 to Toronto, Ontario from Montreal, Quebec, where I was born and lived most of my life, I was surprised to find that my beloved, well-used typewriter would no longer suffice. Not if I wanted my copy to present a current image. So I was kindly informed by a colleague who wanted to help me "integrate" into the Torontonian professional milieu.

Not long before, I had toured the offices of a major Montreal newspaper with a writers' group. There was still only one computer in the news office, which we regarded with great respect as we were given an informational talk on how the newspaper's environment (still full of typewriters just like mine) would not only soon become replete with computers, but it would also become paperless. Shock and awe!

But in business-like Toronto offices, the computers were already there. Everywhere. It didn't take long to become "hooked." How had I lived for so many years without a computer? Clueless at first, I had taken reciprocal lessons from an Israeli computer genius who needed English lessons for his young (hyperactive) daughter. So we traded expertise.

At that time, I was learning on a desktop computer program that my genius teacher had installed on the second-hand computer I acquired from him, and I still appreciate the invaluable advice he gave me: "Don't read a manual," he said. "Never. Learn from the machine. Press all the keys, one by one, and it will teach you everything. Don't be afraid. Nothing will happen. If you make a mistake, you can fix the code." In those days, the visual miracle of drop-down menus had not yet arrived on the personal market. Before this major innovation, you still had to press "Reveal Codes," and lo and behold, a mathematical vision appeared on the computer screen. The code underlying the keys. So you learned to "fix" things by learning to read the code to a degree and deleting the mistakes you had made. Who knew then that in the twenty-first century some people would be cyber-hacking into computer codes for nefarious reasons?

Then around 1990, everything changed again. Now there was a new imperative with that world-changing vehicle, The World Wide Web. Now I could put my writing business on the Web, and suddenly people all over the world could access it. The Internet. Accessible with a few keystrokes. Who needed an office anymore?

Twenty-seven years had elapsed by the time I found myself on this cruise in the South Pacific. I couldn't imagine life now without my computer and cell phone. Neither could my daughter, Susan, who had accompanied me. Unfortunately, although she had purchased an Internet package for use onboard, it was almost impossible to "connect" amid the rolling waves. Even when occasionally we did, the connection was so slow that we couldn't finish a single email before it was "lost" once again. The ocean simply wouldn't cooperate. No Internet. No cell phone. And you can't go to a technical fix-it store for help in the middle of the Pacific Ocean.

We didn't exactly have a funeral for our lost access, but we did have to adjust to life unwired, however temporary. It was a twenty-five-day cruise.

And then we landed on one of the eighty islands of Vanuatu, sixty-five of which are uninhabited. These once volcanic islands are located in Oceania between Australia and Hawaii. In fact, they are about 1,000 miles east of Australia, and closest to New Caledonia, the Fiji islands, the Solomon Islands, and New Guinea. Over the years, the Vanuatu islands have been plagued by large earthquakes, danger of tsunamis, and repeated cyclones. But they are gorgeous, surrounded by turquoise waters, and fine sandy beaches. It's small wonder that when the first people arrived there some 4,000 years ago, they stayed. Unfortunately, they were decimated by disease once the Europeans arrived. In 1606, the Portuguese explorer, Pedro Fernandez de Quiros, sighted these islands, which he called *Espiritu Santu*. By the time Captain James Cook found them in 1774, he renamed them the New Hebrides. In the 1800s, traders arrived to exploit the island's fragrant sandalwood. Then, for a long time, the New Hebrides were under British and French control. With the advent of World War II in the 1940s, the Americans arrived, and in the 1980s, the Republic of Vanuatu emerged as a parliamentary republic.

It was at the most southern of the islands of this Republic that our cruise ship docked. Popularly called Mystery Island, it is uninhabited, and its real name is *Inyeug* (which is close to the main island, *Aneityum*). Islanders refuse to live in *Inyeug* because they believe it is inhabited by ghosts. Even today. Although a few entrepreneurial islanders will come to sell trinkets to tourists by day, at night they have all vanished. The tourists have returned to their cruise ships. It's eerily dark on Mystery Island.

Of course, our ship arrived there in daylight. When we disembarked, we were informed that we could walk around this entire island paradise in less than an hour—forty-five minutes perhaps. So I set out with my daughter, and as we "oohed" and "aahed" our way around the flora of this beautiful, empty place, her phone pinged. A ping in the middle of an uninhabited island in the South Pacific, one that might even be haunted? Did we hear right?

Amazed, my daughter picked up her cellphone. "Hello," said the person calling her from California. "Good to hear your voice." What??? There was reception on the island??? There must be a cell phone tower somewhere nearby. How could it be?

That's when, halfway around the island, we noticed that a modest grass airstrip ran along one part of the beach to the other side. Planes could land here too! As my daughter continued her business conversation with the US, we learned that some of the islands of Vanuatu had been used for the remote locations of a popular television series with instant name recognition everywhere.

Mystery Island was a mystery no more. Modern civilization had been here. It pinged.

SECTION TWO

Australia

Section 2, Australia
The magnificent Great Synagogue in Sydney, Australia, established
in the early 1870s, still maintains services and takes pride in
providing information about Jewish history in Australia.
Photo credit: Susan Spiegel©2015

Raisin Bread and Hot Chocolate

*L*ike the United States or Canada, Australia spans a vast territory. Prior to the devastating bush fires of 2019-2020, I toured much of Australia. May the courage and optimism of its people restore this beautiful land.

When my four children were growing up in the 1970s, our family took lengthy road trips all over North America. Over several years, we visited every single province in Canada—our goal was to reach the Easternmost tip in St. John, Newfoundland and, the next year, the Westernmost tip in Tofino, Vancouver Island (our hardy, beige and brown station wagon traversing log roads stretched over canyons, our luggage doing a balancing act atop the car). "Don't look at the scenery," we would call out to my husband, who was driving. "We'll watch the scenery. Just keep your eye on the road!"

Then, over the next couple of years, we tackled the expansive landscape of the United States. We were already familiar with much of the Eastern seaboard, all the way from Montreal, Quebec in Canada to the east coast of Florida, but now our goal was to visit forty-eight of the fifty states. Only after most of our family had moved to Los Angeles, California did I have the opportunity to visit Alaska and Hawaii to make fifty.

And not until many years later, as rabbi on a cruise ship, did I get to learn words like "Oceania" (an immense, arbitrarily defined expanse of the world where the Pacific Ocean—rather than land borders—connects the nations) and "Australasia"(a region within Oceania that consists of Australia, New Zealand, New Guinea, and the neighboring islands of the South Pacific Ocean). Finally, there was Australia, so like North America in its grand assortment of gorgeous landscapes and diversity of people. So like Canada in many ways, with a history linked to Britain. I felt at home in Australia.

On arrival, though, I was taken aback by the graphic signs in the bathrooms at customs; the signs instructed visitors to sit down on the toilet seats with their feet on the floor, and NOT to place their feet on the toilet seats and squat. For some Oceanic or Australasian countries, even those with relatively modern plumbing, toilets are holes in the floor.

I was surprised, too, by the people just ahead of me who tried to smuggle in food (there are stiff fines for doing so) like raw veal and even a whole, plastic-wrapped, cooked duck in their suitcases. They didn't see anything wrong with it. "If I pay the fine, can I keep the duck?" one young man (an exchange student) asked. He was bringing the duck to his relatives in Australia. No, he couldn't, was the answer.

Maggots were already infesting the bottom of the suitcase belonging to the middle-aged lady who was bringing in veal as a present for her friend who had a restaurant in Sydney. "My friend will cook it for me," the lady explained with a winning smile. But the customs officials confiscated the suitcase, maggots and all, anyway.

Visitors don't have to worry about finding food in Australia. It is readily obtainable in all price ranges, fresh and delicious. But I must say that everywhere I went, it was the raisin bread and hot chocolate I first tasted in the rolling Blue Mountains that made me feel totally at home.

The Blue Mountains are a two-hour or so bus trip from Sydney. Our plans included a cable car over a spectacular canyon, a trip to a recommended animal park featuring kangaroos, wallabies (smaller than kangaroos), monkeys, sloths, and, of course, koala bears. Then we were to take a small boat trip back to Sydney Harbor.

Amid all this scenic grandeur, it was the charming town of Laurel in the heart of the Blue Mountains that captured my heart. The atmosphere is traditional in a way that evokes the English cottage country in earlier times, almost Victorian in feeling. In that little town was a shop that sold soaps and perfumes and a whole repertoire of romantic items, things that had pretty little flowers all over them. I purchased a sturdy shower cap that looked like a Victorian night cap; it had delicate mauve and pink flowers on it too.

Conveniently situated next to this shop was a small café. It was not yet lunchtime, but we had risen early, and we were hungry. I will never forget my first taste of Australian, perfectly toasted raisin bread. It was sliced like a Jewish mother would slice *challah* (there were two slices), an inch thick and lathered with butter. Accompanying it was the best hot chocolate I have ever had. Not cocoa. Not packaged hot chocolate from a processed powder. No, this was thick hot chocolate *sauce* topped off with absolutely delicious, warmed, whole milk from Blue Mountain, grass-fed, Australian cows. Then this gorgeous concoction was well mixed, not in a blender but by hand, to perfection, and, in something approaching ecstasy, I finished it to the last drop. If ever the perfect, mythical red heifer the ancient Jews sought for Temple rites is found, it will be in Australia.

I was hooked. I kept ordering raisin bread and butter and hot chocolate all over Australia, and not once was I disappointed. Better yet, we did so much walking that I didn't gain weight!

A Jewish "First Lady"?

*N*aturally, Susan and I couldn't "see" all of Australia in the brief eight days we were touring there. Or to know it beyond a few choice locales. It would be like claiming familiarity in a week with the vast but disparate territories that make up the US or Canada. But there were certainly many unforgettable moments, enough to make us want to return for more.

Who could forget sailing into Sydney harbor at sunrise? We rose at 5 AM in order not to miss the sunrise, and, as we stepped onto the ship's top deck, already crowded with passengers who didn't want to miss it either, we gasped at the first sight of perhaps the most beautiful harbor in the world, yet strangely reminiscent in its early morning, ethereal beauty of Vancouver's equally breath-taking harbor in Canada. As a matter of fact, I thought fondly of Canada throughout my visit to Australia. Both countries were historically colonies of Great Britain in the time of its proud, great Empire. Both are now independent countries, of course; yet I felt an almost automatic kinship to Australians, both of us retaining more than a little bit of Brit "keep your chin up" in us.

It was not such a happy entry into Australia for England's Esther Abrahams, in 1787. But she did keep her chin up, despite her disastrous early history. Her story is so well known in Australia that her portrait looks out at visitors today at the Jewish Museum in Sydney. Tourist brochures mention her. The Museum guides talk about her. The Old Synagogue hands out printed information. Internet sites record her story.

At the age of fifteen, unmarried and recently pregnant, she was convicted at London's infamous Old Bailey courtroom of stealing twenty-four yards of silk lace and sentenced to seven years transportation to Australia, where she would work as a convict. She sailed there on Lady Penrhyn, one the First Fleet's six ships of convicts, certainly not in the luxurious comfort my daughter and I experienced on our cruise ship, but below the waterline with the portholes bleakly boarded up, and along with 262 other convicts, fifteen of them Jewish. Of the 582 convicts aboard the first six ships, 193 were women. And, of all the convicts shipped to Australia in the years transportation as a sentence was in force, an estimated seven percent of them were Jewish.[3] Some of them were part of Australia's first police force, which was made up largely of convicts.

It would have been a sad immersion indeed for Esther Abrahams into the hardships—rape, among other things—that female convicts faced in colonial Australia if she had not encountered a young marine lieutenant, the well-born George Johnson, aboard the ship; his duties took him down below to keep order. Since she was a most attractive young lady, with lots of curly, black hair, an oval face, a rather long nose, and a rosebud mouth, and he was twenty-three, he promptly fell in love with her. He even purchased a nanny goat at one of the stops so that Esther's newborn, Roseanna, could have milk.[4] She was to become his "de facto" wife when they landed, and—since she had plenty of brains as well as beauty—they accumulated large financial holdings, He finally married her some twenty-five years later. In the interim, they had seven children together.

Although Johnson was later court-martialed for his part in the mutiny against the colony's infamous governor, William Bligh, he was cleared of most of the charges. For six months, in fact, he served as the acting Governor of the colony in Bligh's stead. And that is how, Esther Abrahams, former Jewish felon, became the "First Lady" of Australia for a short time. It is said that she wisely kept herself in the background.

After Johnson died, he left his extensive property to Esther; after her death, it was to go to his children. Unfortunately, her eldest son couldn't wait for that eventuality, and it resulted in unsavory litigation; he tried to declare her senile. She spent her last years living quietly in the home of her youngest son, David. Some of her descendants became influential leaders in Australia.

The Opera Glasses: Seeing Through a Glass Clearly

*L*ong ago, when I was a star-struck teenager in Montreal, I would attend matinees on Wednesday afternoons. On these theatrical expeditions, I was accompanied by my mother who considered it "cultural enrichment"—her notes to my teachers on Thursday mornings always attributed my absences to a cold. Usually we would go to "His Majesty's Theatre." When Queen Elizabeth ascended to the throne, it became "Her Majesty's Theatre," but we sat in the same seats. Since we were frequent attendees, and my mother's budget was small, we sat in the top balcony (many aspiring actors were there too). In order to see the players' features clearly, what were then called "opera glasses"—although these plays weren't opera, they were often "musicals"—were a boon.

So one of my first purchases, once I became a teenage radio actress actually earning a paycheck, was a pair of elegant opera glasses. Not any old opera glasses; these were black mother-of-pearl, delicately shaped and gold rimmed. They had their own silk cord so the opera glasses could rest around my neck, as well as a silk pouch to house them. They were mine for many years until a house robbery made them the illicit property of someone else. I missed them. They were a happy memory of my youth.

Not until I glimpsed the architectural marvel of the Opera House in Sydney, Australia, not until we toured these magically-conceived premises, did I re-experience the excitement of the curtain going up at Her Majesty's Theatre. The dramatic sections of the Opera House, like the winged shells of a concrete sea creature, rise from the sea, occupying all of Bennelong Point at Sydney Harbor.

The Sydney Opera House, which finally opened in 1973 after a lengthy gestation period beginning with an architectural competition in 1957, was designed by Danish architect Jorn Utzon. As a distinctive, multi-purpose, performing arts venue, it was declared a World Heritage Site in 2007. I consider it to be one of the wonders of the world.

And there, in the lobby's boutique, I found the replacement for my long-lost opera glasses. No matter that they were amber-colored, not pearl. They were delicately-shaped; they had a gold rim and cord. I would cherish them as a forever remembrance of Australia.

Although I usually purchase better seating when I go to the theatre today and don't really need opera glasses, they symbolize a part of who I am. They recall a time when I was young and in love with the theatre, when life held great artistic momentum; they were an inspirational part of my route to eventually becoming a rabbi. They also symbolize the beauty, elegance, and sophistication of Sydney itself. A city to cherish and revisit, marked by engaging architecture; arched, fashionable shopping malls; quality food and merchandise. It was also full of tourists, and costs for food and shelter were staggeringly high. Many people who "live in Sydney" today actually live in the suburbs, which we couldn't get to explore in the time we had at our disposal. We were told that the suburbs are beautiful too. And also expensive. If you visit Sydney, it will cost you, especially the hotels.

My new opera glasses were certainly a cut above the room we, my daughter and I, had reserved for our stay there. When we were choosing our hotel from Los Angeles, with the help of a reputable travel agent, we asked to keep our costs "reasonable"; he suggested that we might enjoy the vibrancy of the Chinese section of Sydney. "The hotel is modest," he said, "but it's an exciting part of town. Lots of great restaurants. Interesting art. Diversity." All of that proved to be true, but he had never been there. What he didn't know was that the "basic" hotel he booked for us stood right next to one that boasted a large sign: "Rooms by the hour." And there were others quite similar. How basic can you get?

Actually, it proved to be great fun to walk around savoring the sights and sounds of "Chinatown." In a sense, it was familiar territory. Every metropolitan North American city that I've lived in had a big Chinese population and a resultant popular Chinatown. Although most people of Chinese background don't live in Sydney's Chinatown anymore, the tourist attractions, the food, and the businesses remain. Our hotel proved to be a moderately lengthy but pleasant walk to the harbor, where our activities for the day—and the Opera House—were located. It's easy to spend an entire day at the harbor. If you have the physical energy, as many athletic visitors do, you can climb the walking path of the bridge high enough to gain an amazing view. Half-way up, there is a small museum. My daughter climbed. I watched.

Now that we had our bearings in Sydney (we gauged distance from the harbor), I checked out the location of the historical Old Synagogue (also known as the Great Synagogue), and the times when we could visit. Along with the Jewish Museum, a much newer edifice, that would be my destination for the next day. Even if you don't visit a religious establishment, a trip to Australia brings you close to God.

The Great Jewish Synagogue is Still Great

*I*t's an old Jewish joke that when there are two Jews, three synagogues are needed. They each have their own ideas about how the prayers should be conducted. Prior to visiting the Great Synagogue in Sydney, Australia, I left a message identifying myself as an ordained rabbi from Los Angeles who was interested in the synagogue's history. I don't know which of the two or more Jews got my message, but no one seemed to be aware of it when I arrived. However, at least there was a synagogue to receive me, a grand one. Often referred to as "The Jewish Cathedral," it was established in 1878.[5]

But a hundred years earlier in 1788, when the first few Jewish convicts were transported to New South Wales on the First Fleet to serve out their harsh sentences, there were no synagogues yet, not even one. As a matter of fact, when the first Jewish convict died that same year, there were no Jewish burial rites or sites.[6]

Although only ten Jews are required to make a *minyan* (while each person can pray individually, developing communal values is considered essential in Jewish life, and the Torah cannot be read aloud without a *minyan*), the idea is to gather enough participants to make a *kehilla*, a little community. Eventually—some three decades later—there were enough Jewish convicts—about thirty of them—to gather together for regular worship. Towards the end of the 1820s, a few free settlers joined the congregation as well, led by a young man recommended by the Chief Rabbi in London.[7]

So now there was one synagogue for thirty plus Jews. *Oy veh!* That wouldn't do. They argued and argued about different ways of conducting services in the synagogue. And other things. It goes without saying that

27

a rival congregation was immediately started, led by a young man who *didn't* have a recommendation from London. Who cared? Now they had two synagogues. The number of free Jewish settlers grew. After a lot of negotiation, and helped by a rabbi who had traveled to Australia, the two congregations united. They were one.

It turned out that some of the free Jewish settlers had influential ties (to the Montefiore family, for example), and the Australian government finally recognized the Jewish congregation in 1831. The little congregation celebrated their first High Holy Days together a few months later on George Street in a room above the store of one of the congregants. There was a *bona fide* Jewish congregation in New South Wales, Australia.[8]

From this small beginning, under the leadership of their first actual rabbi, Rev. Michael Rose, the congregation grew to 300 people and soon had to take larger facilities on Bridge Street and then, only a decade later, on York Street, in a 500-seat building designed by James Hume.[9] By this time, non-Jews were also taking interest in the synagogue and contributing to the project. Amazing.

What had boosted the Jewish population and made this phenomenal growth possible? The Gold Rush of the 1850s attracted a surge of enterprising settlers, a number of Jews who were all free settlers among them. Unfortunately, their different circumstances led to conflict between the old and new settlers so that—you guessed it!—a rival synagogue was again established.

Finally, almost a century after the first Jewish convict died in Australia without Jewish burial rites, the rival synagogues united once again, and the Great Synagogue was born on Elizabeth Street, where it still stands.[10] The religious services, complemented by fine liturgical talent, were—and still are—traditional in nature.

In the formal and elegant fashion of the time, the Great Synagogue was built to generate awe at its stately magnificence, both outside and inside. There are stained glass windows and gold stars (added in later years) on the ceiling to intensify the light. It's gorgeous. An education center, auditorium, memorial center, and library were added over the years. The Great Synagogue still boasts many activities, but the elderly volunteers told us that the whole congregation is aging and, by attrition, dwindling.

As my visit drew to a close, I noticed that there were *mincha* (afternoon) services scheduled for 1:30 PM. "I'd love to join in prayer at the *mincha* service," I said to the knowledgeable woman who gave us an informational talk. "Would that be possible?" I asked.

"Well, it's usually just the men," she answered hesitantly, and then added, "I suppose we could put up a screen for you."

"Thank you," I replied, "but since my time in Sydney is short, I think it would be better spent at the Jewish Museum than behind a screen."

Oh, that's great," she said in relief. "There's a bus that will take you to the Museum that stops right in front of our door."

So with an exchange of smiles and good wishes, my daughter and I left for the Jewish Museum of Sydney, where I promptly bought a purple *kippah* (head covering) with an aboriginal design.

With the dispersion of young families to the more affordable suburbs around Sydney, there are a number of thriving, suburban synagogues today—Reform, Conservative, and Modern Orthodox—and most have egalitarian seating. Female rabbis who visit Sydney are not obliged to sit behind a *mechitza* (screen or wall) in order to pray there, if they do not so choose.

So you see, the old maxim is true. When you have two Jews, you need three synagogues.

The Brave—and Smart—Little Penguins

*W*ho would have thought that politically correct terminology would extend to the little penguins of Phillip Island, Victoria province, just a couple of hours driving time from the city of Melbourne? In Australia, where my daughter, Susan, and I were spending a few precious tourist days, these little penguins were formerly called "fairy penguins" because of their small size. The smallest species of penguin (*Eudyptula minor*), about thirteen inches in height and seventeen inches in length, they can be found on the coastlines of Southern Australia and New Zealand. Phillip Island is said to be home to about 33,000 breeding adults, its one remaining penguin colony.

To me, a "fairy" conjures up the delicate creatures with gossamer wings that populated my story books when I was a child. Or the cartoon fairies in Walt Disney movies. But, owing to sensitivity to the LGBTQ+ movement, in recent years the "fairy" penguins are referenced in public documents as "little penguins." Their Maori name is *korora*.

In any case, they are much, much smaller than the Emperor penguins of the Antarctic, whose lifestyles were captured in *The March of the Penguins*, an awe-inspiring 2005 documentary that caught the popular imagination. The Emperor Penguins sported black and white feathers, but these little penguins in Australia are blue and white—blue-feathered, to camouflage them from land-predators by blending into the deep blue sea where they spend 80 percent of their time foraging for food for their babies; and white-bellied to protect them from predators swimming below them in the sea. They are the only penguins in the world with blue and white outer feathers, which they keep waterproof by preening (and adding a drop of oil onto every feather from a special gland above the tail). Their feathers adapt into flippers for swimming.

Realizing how unique these penguins are, Penguin Island officials provide a way for interested tourists to watch the nightly parade of little penguins emerging from the sea —a ritual that occurs only at sunset and always at sunset, every day. Visitors must order tickets in advance that allow them to sit on benches set not too close to the sea in order not to scare the penguins but still close enough to see them well. As visitors, Susan and I had to arrive and be seated early for the same reason.

Oh, it is so cold and windy out there on the beach. The sea is freezing cold too. The penguins like it that way. My daughter and I huddled up close to one another in jackets and hats and blankets, but the sea mist and the wind cut right through. Our fingers and toes froze. Only a few hours earlier we had been in warm and welcoming Melbourne. But we had come too far to retreat to the bus.

It was well worth it though, the experience of a true natural marvel as we watched the little penguins become partly visible, almost separating themselves from the waves one at a time, looking around to see if other penguins had arrived yet, and then ducking back into the sea to wait for the safety of additional penguin company before they braved the land.

There was reason to be fearful. Predators in the form of large land-birds – sometimes there are feral dogs or cats as well—were already circling the shore in anticipation of the penguins' sunset arrival. So the little penguins waited. There would be safety in numbers. You couldn't help but marvel at the wonders of God's world as more and more penguins appeared in ones and twos and threes. Finally there were enough to get into formation.

Instinctively they formed a little, single-file army, one brave penguin leading. One after another, they marched, following the penguin ahead in a straight line, no penguin diverging, and, once back in the grasses that lined the shore, they hurried directly to their individual burrows (little Australian penguins live in burrows). The land-birds did not have the temerity to attack such a formidable-appearing force, even if individually each penguin was only a little over a foot tall.

How did the little penguins know where to go once they crossed the beach to the grasses that lined the shore? They were directed by the cries of their babies. To our human ears, all of them seemed to be crying out to their mothers together in one huge cacophony of wails. But just as a human mother somehow recognizes the cry of her own baby, so the penguins could identify the sound of their own. And they went straight to where their male partners were still guarding the babies. It was a moment not to be missed.

How do you tell the girls from the boys? The males have a little extra hook on their beaks. They are the ones that guard the babies in their burrows while the females are in the sea for long days, gorging themselves on seafood so that they will able to feed their babies. It's an interesting feeding mechanism, kind of like an internal blender with a spout. They simply regurgitate the food from their beaks into their baby penguins' hungry mouths. Economical and efficient. Soon the wails on Phillip Island ceased.

Little penguins don't necessarily mate for life; it depends on the breeding success of the couples in producing eggs. Divorce rates may run up to fifty percent. Normally, the females lay two eggs (about the size of chicken eggs), with an incubation period of thirty-five days. Yes, both parents take turns in incubating their eggs. Then the little ones head out to sea when they are between seven to eleven weeks old. And they know what to do! As if they were touched by a fairy wand! Or the hand of the Creator.

SECTION THREE

Brazil, South America

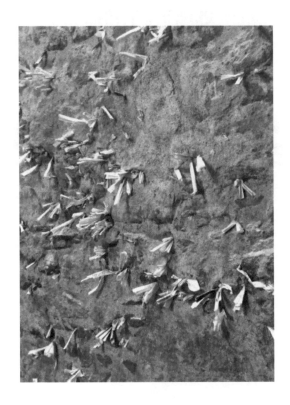

Section 3, Brazil, South America
In Recife, Brazil, visitors place written prayers in the crevices of a replica of Jerusalem's Wailing Wall at the *Sinagoga Kahal Zur Israel* complex. The original synagogue was established in 1636.
Photo credit: Susan Spiegel©2016

The Sands of Time

*I*n one year alone, I spent one hundred days at sea visiting disparate parts of the world. I have now conducted all the *Chags* (Jewish Festivals), as well as many Sabbaths and some Interfaith services on the ocean in many lands, and it has been a life-changing experience in terms of my feeling of connection to Jews, past and present everywhere.

It was so moving, for example, to stand in the beautifully restored old synagogue (established in 1636 as the *Kahal Zur Israel* Synagogue) in Recife, Brazil. Originally, the synagogue had sand floors, one of five in the world. I realized that I was standing where, centuries ago, twenty-three courageous Jewish people departed from this congregation, fleeing persecution from the Inquisition that had travelled from Europe to Brazil. It was the second time they were fleeing the Inquisition; in 1497, they had already escaped the Inquisition in Portugal for what they hoped was safety in a new, faraway land. That land was Brazil (colonized by the Dutch until the Portuguese defeated them).

The Jewish refugees originally came in the guise of New Christians or *Conversos*, but secretly most of them practiced Judaism and married only within their own group. Now, with the emergence of this threat of the new Inquisition, a small group risked sailing to Peter Stuyvesant's fledgling New Amsterdam, where they pleaded for admittance as refugees. That is how Jewish people who did not want to live in hiding or masked as Christians, as many others did, but rather continue to conduct their lives by the Holy Laws of Judaism, came to dwell in what was to be New York in America.

Other secret Jews fled to Curacao, where there is a second

sand-floor synagogue (*Mikve Israel Emmanuel*) in Willemstad, where I also visited. With about 200 congregants today, it was built in 1732 by the descendants of the Jews who fled there. Others fled to areas of the Caribbean.

That is why three more synagogues with sand floors can also be found in Kingston, Jamaica; Saint Thomas, Virgin Islands; and Paramaribo, Suriname (the latter is technically in South America). They still maintain the sand-floor tradition.

Why did these Portuguese secret Jews fleeing the Inquisition put sand on the floor of their synagogues? The reasons given are symbolic. First of all, the sand was to remind them of the forty years the biblical Israelites had spent wandering in the desert. Secondly, it was a reminder of how their Portuguese ancestors had placed sand on the floor of their basement synagogues in Portugal to muffle the sound of their sacred rituals.

In 1665, the Portuguese, who had by now defeated the Dutch, closed the *Kahal Zur Israel* Synagogue in Recife and expelled 1,200 Jews. Judaism was banned. Although since the early 1900s, Jews have once again prospered in Brazil, it was not until 2002 that the synagogue's doors reopened for the first time since the seventeenth century.[11] It had been closed for 347 years. It is said to be the oldest existing synagogue in the Americas. In the US, the oldest shul is the *Touro* Synagogue in Newport, Rhode Island.

And in the winter of 2016, when I traveled from Brazil to Willemstad, Curacao, where other members of the old Recife congregation had fled, I took my shoes off in the sanctuary of *Mikve Israel Emmanuel* and stood gratefully in prayer. On the sand floor.

Follow the *Mikveh! Kali Zur Israel* Synagogue

*H*ave you ever immersed yourself in a *mikveh*? Probably not, unless you are an orthodox Jew. Modern *mikvehs* look like what would be a very tiny swimming pool in Los Angeles. Going to the *mikveh* can be a celebratory or purification ritual before the Sabbath, a wedding, recovery from illness, or as part of a conversion ceremony. Men go separately, and religious Jews often do. It is especially an age-old requirement for Jewish women, as a kind of ritual purification after menstruation or the birth of a child. Immersion in the *mikveh*—you have to be squeaky clean before you descend its steps into the water. There are attendants to help you, like a spa. You recite beautiful prayers and feel wonderful afterwards. If it's a conversion, the supporting rabbi will accompany you.

I immersed completely in the *mikveh*—the day before I was ordained as a rabbi—not a strand of hair can show above the water. I'm not orthodox. You don't have to be orthodox to go to the *mikveh*. If you can't swim, the attendant will kneel beside the pool and hold your hand.

There are strict standards to maintain, though. The *mikveh's* water must be natural, spotlessly clean, and constantly circulating from a fresh source (oceans, rivers, spring-fed lakes, even rainwater or ice or snow collected to meet specific transport and handling regulations). It is usually housed in an enclosed space either built into the ground or attached to a building. It can't be a portable arrangement. Most *mikvehs* today have water-purification and filtration systems, which makes the plumbing expensive to maintain.

Alternatively, you can simply immerse yourself completely in the sea three times and say the prayers, but there is the danger of currents sweeping you away, and the weather doesn't always cooperate. So *mikvehs* are usually indoors. Of course, with indoor plumbing, hot water, and even luxury bathtubs available in North America today, many Jewish women no longer feel the need to go to the *mikveh*. Like an appendix, it seems unnecessary, an anachronism.

But the *mikveh* is not just about cleanliness of the body. It's not a bath. You have to take a bath or shower and clip your nails BEFORE you enter the *mikveh* squeaky clean. There is a strong spiritual dimension involved. It's a Jewish RITUAL bath, in which you immerse ALL of you. Three times, and with each immersion you say a special prayer, ending with the core Hebrew prayer, the *Shema* ("Hear O Israel, the Lord our God, the Lord is One"). Guests may sit behind a screen and offer prayers and blessings, even songs, as well. It's an occasion.

And where there is a *mikveh*, you can be sure there will be a synagogue. Some people say, "Follow the money!" In this case, you can say, "Follow the *mikveh*!" That's why people in Brazil were so excited when a centuries-old *mikveh* was discovered in Recife in the year 2000. Interested archeologists, who already possessed old maps and records, had started to dig—eight floors down—beneath a building in the old Street of the Jews (*Rua dos Judeus*). And they found it! So they knew. That's where the oldest synagogue in the Americas had once been.

Yes, it was the site of the old *Kahal Zur Israel* Synagogue, founded in 1630.[12] A congregation of Jewish refugees from the Inquisition in Europe had prayed there until the conquering Portuguese banned Judaism in Brazil. So by 1654, the Jews were forced to flee again. Or else to hide their religion as *Conversos*, sometimes in the interior wilds of Brazil. Eventually, they created prosperous sugar plantations and other thriving businesses and are credited with building up the economy of Brazil in many ways.

Although many Brazilian Jews left for Israel in 1948, about 120,000 Jews still populate Brazil today, largely centered in the big cities of Sao Paulo or Rio de Janeiro, home of *Carnival*. Unfortunately, in recent years, there has been some anti-Israel sentiment in Brazil, with some officials holding strong pro-Palestinian views.

But the Jewish community is still strong. And today, directly across the street from the recently rebuilt *Kahal Zur Israel* (which means "Rock of Israel community") Synagogue in Recife stands a Jewish museum and cultural center. What makes the complex extraordinary is that part of the excavated *mikveh* is on display right there—protectively covered by glass. It was this ritual bath's discovery that reactivated philanthropic interest in rebuilding the old synagogue in the spot where it once stood.

Although the museum and cultural center are stunningly beautiful, throughout the time I was there, my eyes kept returning to the excavated *mikveh*; my heart was in the *mikveh*, my thoughts spilling into its protected waters.

In Los Angeles, where I live, I serve from time to time as a *dayan* (judge) in a rabbinic court—one of the three rabbis that make up a *Beit Din* (House of Justice). After a conversion acceptance, it is a joyful part of our task to accompany the applicant to the *mikveh* to complete the conversion process. For me, each time it is a mystical moment, connecting all of those present to the divine. Each time I have tears in my eyes, just as I did looking into this *mikveh* dating back to the 1600s—and excavated at the very beginning of the third millennium in what, for me, no longer felt like a foreign land.

Carnival—A Lifeline in Rio

All the way along the coast to Rio de Janeiro, we could see the progress of the world-renowned *Carnival* in the small towns and cities near our ports of call. Early on, stands were already being constructed; a little later, decorations were being added, parts of costumes tried on, carried on hangers, even worn in the streets in each of the places we stopped. Every Brazilian town of any size, at least on the east coast, has its own *Carnival*.

It's not just a once a year performance that's at stake; it's a progression towards the ultimate by the inhabitants of Brazil, toward maybe being the best samba dancers, musicians, and artists in the land. The Rio de Janeiro show will be attended by thousands of tourists—and, of course, proud Brazilians.

As we sailed up the coast of Brazil, we could see the grim signs of poverty too, the ugly graffiti that deface once beautiful buildings and the grey, broken-down *favelas* (miserable slums occupied by squatters) that, ghostlike, ring big cities like Rio. Of course, the city also boasts areas where the rich live, like the luxury apartments and big hotels surrounding the fabled Copacabana Beach (reminiscent of Miami) or the magnificent mansions around the site of the historic Imperial Palace. As the English Charles Dickens wrote in a Victorian context, it's a tale of two cities.

However, in Brazil you can't always tell the income level of an area by what appears outside. It's common for residents not to keep the exteriors in good repair to avoid paying extra taxes. Inside, the apartments may be very nicely furnished and well kept.

The *favelas*, though, are completely run-down; the front yards are rubble, where children play and teenagers flirt. Because these areas are a jumble of lanes without addresses where mail can be delivered (at least, at the time I was there), the socialist government (no longer in power) was providing free telephone service and Internet access to the residents. Despite the pervading poverty, it seemed like most everyone had—or had access to—a smart phone.

Portuguese-speaking, local taxi drivers who couldn't speak English used cell phones as portable translators; the customers spoke English into the phone, and it was translated into Portuguese; and vice versa.

"I'm sorry I don't speak English," the driver apologized.

"I'm sorry I don't speak Portuguese," I replied (that is, Portuguese, Brazilian style, with guttural sounds far removed from Portuguese, Portugal style).

Yet somehow we communicated very well. It's amazing how far cell phones and hand gestures can take you. Plus the limited phrases from our guide book (and the couple of classes in getting-to-know Portuguese that we took on the ship) helped us as we drove around the city.

Rio is undoubtedly well guarded. Standing over Rio, its huge, art-deco-style dimensions and outstretched arms protecting the city, is the iconic statue of Christ the Redeemer. Standing atop a pedestal on the summit of Mount Corcovado, and made of reinforced concrete covered with thousands of triangular pieces of soapstone, it is ninety-eight feet tall; the reach of its extended arms is ninety-two feet. Since 2007, it has been considered one of the Seven New Wonders of the World. Although it's by far the largest statue of Christ in the world, Catholic monuments and churches of varying sizes and splendor can be found everywhere throughout Brazil.

"Thank God that the people have the Church and *Carnival*," I remarked to the cruise ship's Catholic priest. "I think they would explode without them." The tension in the country, centering on the need for jobs in the face of big projects stalled everywhere for lack of money, is palpable. At each of the ship's stops, young men stood in groups, arms grimly folded, eyes devouring us, hoping for work that wasn't there for them.

It is a syncretic kind of religion, though, that colors *Carnival*. Some Brazilian natives (especially in the north of Brazil, closest to the US) had been slaves, transported to this country from Africa by colonial powers to work in the plantations and mines. Despite the best efforts of Christian missionaries, Brazilians throughout the country still retain vestiges of the native religions that once permeated the jungle areas. Although eventually most converted to Christianity, they superimposed their native deities on top of the Christian trinity and saints. It makes for a very vibrant, transposed religion in many keys that dances its way to the competitions of *Carnival.*

Carnival is so integral to the spirit of Brazil that I had always thought it was run by the government, but this is not so. Apparently, it is a private, year-long enterprise. It organizes samba clubs all over Brazil that develop their own routines, different each year, and practice hard and long to enter their own club's "show" in competition. Eventually twelve and then six samba clubs are chosen. These are invited to design their décor and sew their costumes in a specially constructed complex in Rio.

It is these six clubs that finally perform at *Carnival*, and thousands of people, many of them tourists, attend. Each club performs for an hour and a half in one night's frenzied entertainment. So with six clubs performing, that's a total of nine continuous hours that audiences sit on concrete benches to applaud the frenetic dancers and musicians. (By the time we got to Rio, tickets were $500 per person to sit on the backless benches; if you wanted a reserved seat with a back and a little closer to the entertainment, the tickets were $1,000 apiece.) The very next day there is a free *Carnival* parade for the populace led by the winning club.

Our ship had arranged for local dancers and musicians to put on a private, onboard show (beautifully costumed dancers, shaking their almost bare backsides to frenetic rhythms, delighted some of the older men on board by dancing with them). Rather than brave the crowds and continuous alcohol consumption late at night, my daughter and I opted for this shipboard arrangement (it was terrific)! In addition, since many smaller towns also put on a dynamic show, we attended one at the next stop; it was well worth the price ($150 per ticket).

As it happens, the revelry of *Carnival* takes place close to the time of Purim, the Jewish festival where young and old kids dress up as Queen Esther and King Ahasuerus and hiss and shake noise-makers at the villain, Haman, who wanted to kill all the Jews in long-ago Persia. The Festival of Purim, too—the one night of the year Jews are supposed to get drunk!—has acted as a safety valve for the many years that Jewish people suffered persecution at the hands of various countries. People need to let off steam in difficult situations, and a festival of this kind is a joyful way of doing it.

Whatever your religious belief, thank God for Purim, and thank God for *Carnival.* These festivals continue to allow for a reprieve of happiness in the midst of miserable conditions; the concentration of working towards a collective, bigger-than-oneself goal; and the opportunity to be grateful for the vibrancy of life while we live it. They can be a lifeline to better times.

Choosing Your Protein in a Land of Plenty

efore I travelled to Brazil, it never occurred to me how much hard work it takes to get less than a handful of nuts from the nut tree (nuts do grow on trees). They look a lot different in their natural state than they do included in a delectable chocolate bar. First someone agile has to climb the tree; then he (usually) has to chop down the large husk, which falls to the ground. Next the thick, hairy, husk is smashed open (it takes considerable effort—and precision—by a man or woman, a lot more than, say, opening a jar of nuts with elderly hands when you can't remember where you put the jar opener). Inside that inner shell is the core of the husk, and inside that core lies its heart—perhaps four Brazil nuts. That's why they are so expensive when you buy them in a North American supermarket. They'd be a lot more expensive if agricultural labor in Brazil were not so poorly rewarded.

Producing the chocolate (made from cocoa or cocoa beans, which also grow on trees) for the bars is also a lengthy process. The beans, which are the basis of chocolate, have a leathery rind, and the beans inside have to be extracted from the rind, fully fermented, and dried. Because the seed has fat, cocoa butter also can be extracted.

I visited one rural village where the chocolate beans were broken down in the old-fashioned way by a donkey hitched to a small mill. The donkey provided the power as he went round and round as directed. Round and round, over and over. Using more modern methods, the industrialized production of chocolate from cocoa beans is big business today.

I have now visited nut plantations, cocoa plantations, coffee plantations. Some of the processes involve roasting in an open flame oven as well. The number of different products that can be made from these agricultural materials is amazing. But my personal affection is reserved for the coconut. One caveat: if you sit under a coconut tree when the nuts are ripening (that is, the husks are no longer green), it may be your last day on earth should a coconut fall on your head, something that is quite possible. So while you can sit under an apple tree romantically in North America, beware the coconut tree in South America for shading yourself, a seductive option in the tropical heat, to say the least.

As with the Brazil nuts, it's also quite a job to climb a tree and hack down and then open a coconut. However, it's worth the effort because every single part of the coconut can be used. Think of all the ways in which a coconut and its foliage contribute to society.

Actually, it was not in Brazil but rather in one of the Fiji islands in the South Pacific (there are some 330 of them, only about 110 of them inhabited, plus 500 islets) that my love affair with the coconut began. Many of the islanders have very frizzy hair, and some of them still let it grow out wild and bushy. My own hair, which is pleasantly curly in dry Southern California but grows to frizzy proportions in a humid, tropical climate, can actually look quite presentable with daily applications of coconut butter, a product I found commercially from a Fijian company that ships its products all over the world. I slather the coconut butter (really intended as a skin cream) all over my face too. Some of the creams intended to protect your skin from climactic wear cost a lot of money. A word of advice: try coconut.

The people of the Republic of Fiji (for a long time, from 1879 -1970, they were a Crown Colony of Britain) are warriors by nature. Even on their main island, Viti Levu, their small dwellings huddle defensively close together in their villages, despite the fact that there is lots of surrounding land. They maintain a large standing army, of which they are proud—native Fijians have served in major wars and continue to partner with their allies in democratic countries. As small memorials attest, they are proud of their patriotic service.

For many years, Western countries trod lightly when dealing with Fiji—that is, explorers and missionaries avoided going there because of Fiji's history of aggressive cannibalism. In fact, an early missionary's leather shoes that refused to soften in the boiling vat are still on display in the Fiji museum, along with the impressive sea-going vessels that the Fijians crafted to sell (despite the fact that they were not sailors).

Eating their human enemies ritually gave them their enemies' power, they believed. They had special long forks by which they fed their priests in symbolic rituals. This human food did not actually touch the priests' lips—it just slid down their throats. I'm ashamed to say that I bought a tourist version of the ritual fork for my grandson. Better a chocolate bar with Brazil nuts. Or aromatic Brazilian coffee. Or coconut butter face cream from Fiji for his hair (it's curly too).

No one eats another human in Fiji today—and given the multiple benefits derived from the coconut and from the surrounding sea, they really didn't (and don't) need this kind of protein. As a matter of fact, Fiji has one of the most developed economies in the Pacific, with extensive forest, mineral, and fish resources. I must admit, though, that as a first time visitor, I felt a little queasy when I considered that the cannibalistic history of these vigorous islanders was less than a couple of hundred years behind them. As history reminds us from time to time, even in the twenty-first century, civilization can be a thin veneer, indeed.

The Meeting of the Waters

*T*he Amazon River in Brazil boasts 2,500 varieties of fish. I wouldn't recommend putting a hand in its opaque, café au lait colored waters, however. They're not the crystal clear waters of the Bahamas where you can see right down to the white sand. While these waters of the Amazon derive their color from the sandy banks and dense plant life that surround them, they are treacherous. Forget swimming if you are not a native. In fact, the Amazon River abounds with flesh-eating predators.

There are, according to author Matthew Wells, fearsome black caimans with large heads and voracious appetites (often twenty feet long, they have been called "alligators on steroids"); they'll tackle anything as food, a leg here and an arm there, they're not specific). Numerous other dangerous water species abound—ever-hungry fish or reptiles that would be happy to take a chunk out of visitors to their territory.[13]

Also among them are the green Anaconda, reputed to be the largest snakes in the world (some twenty-nine feet long), who prefer the shallow waters where they can constrict and suffocate their victims; the Arapaima, with scary armored scales—and whose tongue also has teeth; Giant Otters, often referred to as "river wolves"; Bull Sharks whose powerful jaws make them one of the most feared attackers; Electric Eels who really kill their prey, hopefully not you, with jolts of electricity; and Piranhas, primarily scavengers known for their feeding frenzies when they are really hungry. The most insidious fish, however, are the *Candiros*. These are small, parasitic, freshwater catfish. Do not, however secretly, urinate in the opaque waters of the Amazon, or these little demons will swim right into your urethra and lodge in the

47

urinary tract. Since they have spines on their backs, it takes surgery to get them out.[14]

Of course, not all of the fish in the Amazon River are predators. Lots of them are prey. Amazingly, despite all the water creatures eager for human food, from time to time, locals can be seen fishing from the shore. If you gotta eat, you gotta eat, I guess. Or maybe they are familiar with the times when the carnivores will most likely be hungry. Sometimes the long arms of a favorite pet of the region, the furry sloth, will be hanging from the necks of these indigenous people. A human, it seems, is just as good as a tree for hanging out.

In any case, there are lots of fish in the Amazon river, and most of them are not flesh-eating. Lots of them prefer seafood to people. Actually, the many diverse species come from the merging of two or more rivers. This merging—when two bodies of water meet (sometimes one of them is a tributary) and then join to become one river—is called a confluence. In the case of the Amazon River in Brazil, the meeting of the waters provides an amazing visual display—it is truly spectacular— as the two streams resist mixing their colors. As they approach one another, the contrast is striking: the dark-hued Rio Negro and the coffee-tone of the Amazon.

The Rio Negro is not really a black river, as its Spanish name would proclaim, but it is a dark color, classed among the blackwaters of the world. It is also a large body of water, in fact the largest tributary of the Amazon. As it enters the Amazon from the left, the Rio Negro insists on keeping its own dark color. So does the pale sandy Rio Solimoes, which continues to flow from the upper part of the Amazon River. They are so stubborn, these rivers. You have to see it to believe it.

I watched in amazement as the two rivers continued to flow in their own streams, at their own levels (the Solimoes flows beside and below the Rio Negro), in their own preferred colors, without mixing. They maintain different temperatures, different speeds, different water density. The Rio Negro flows at near two kilometers per hour (1.2 mph) at a temperature of 28 degrees C (82 degrees F), while the Rio Solimoes flows between four to six kilometers per hour (2.5 to 3.7 mph) at a temperature of 22 degrees C. They are different in the movement of air masses.[15]

Not only do the waters continue to be separatists in the same Amazon river for about six kilometers (3.7 miles), but they also contain different fish—different species—in each of the two streams. They do not mix either; they maintain their own levels in an "us" and "other" situation. A "fishuation," you might say in jest, an almost Talmudic dilemma since each "side" has a different point of view. The Talmud is full of rabbis disagreeing and maintaining their own positions. Usually they find a middle ground.

But if they can't, as the Talmud also teaches, when two forces maintain an oppositional view and refuse to compromise, a third force is needed to "lift them up" from their folly. In other words, two oppositional ideas can generate a third choice that they haven't previously considered. That's what happens in the Amazon River. A huge natural blockage, some six kilometers past their first meeting place near the Brazilian city of Manaus, impedes the river's flow and crunches the two streams together like an oversize mix-master. After that, there are no more distinctive plumes traveling at their own levels, temperatures, and populations. The unfazed Amazon continues its journey—it's one of the longest rivers in the world, rivaling the Nile—as a churning, united muddy brown. In its own way, it's a beautiful, flowing middle ground.

Trinidad and Tobago: A President's Gracious Greeting

*O*n the way home from Brazil, we stopped at the tropical but orderly Caribbean islands of Trinidad and Tobago. What a change from the South American tumult of Brazil in the midst of *Carnival*! Truth to tell, it was a welcome respite. Even getting a taxi in Tobago was pleasant; the taxis lined up in orderly fashion, and the dispatcher sent them off with customers one after another. The driver was courteous and well-informed. The beaches were beautiful, and Tobago is a quiet, relaxing place to take a vacation.

Too soon, we were off to Tobago's twin island, Trinidad, a much more developed place and beautiful in its own way. Although it is evident that business takes place here, the island does not have a commercial but rather a gracious quality. This was evidenced, to our great surprise, by our unexpected but welcoming encounter with the president—yes, the president—of both Trinidad and Tobago. Where? Right in front of his home. Isn't that where presidents are when they are not doing the nation's business?

"Let's see if the president is home," our tour guide suggested enthusiastically. The president's government house was adjacent to the landmark botanical gardens of which Trinidadians are very proud. If you're a tourist to this lovely, sparkling clean tropical island, you're not likely to miss these lush surroundings. The grounds around the president's house were beautifully landscaped too.

"Ooh, I see his car. I think he's home. Let's ask." Just like that. Off our tour guide went to approach the guard post securing the house, as our tour group of some thirty individuals stood with our mouths collectively open at her *chutzpah* (nerve). For a while she conversed with the couple of uniformed guards who were indeed protecting access to the long driveway that led to the president's house. Then, a few moments later, she came back to our group, nodding energetically and smiling.

"They say he's home," she trilled. "And they're going to ask him if he'd like to meet us." In retrospect, it seemed an almost biblical moment. Like when Abraham goes to see King Abimelech (twice), although he is not honest about Sarah being his wife and not his sister. Moses and Aaron go to see the Pharaoh to show off God's power and demand that God's people be set free. If you want to see the king, you go to see the king. Why not? You tell the king what you think and what you want. But we tourists didn't have anything of special importance to communicate or demand. And the president was not exactly a king.

A few members of our sophisticated group thought it was ridiculous to ask the president of the combined country of Trinidad and Tobago to meet our touring group on the spur of the moment. It seemed to them an impossible—even impudent—request. They were embarrassed.

After all, this was a very distinguished president. Why should he bother to make time to see us?

His Excellency Anthony Carmona, SC, ORTT was not only the fifth president of Trinidad and Tobago, in office since 2013, but he had previously served as High Court Judge at the Supreme Court of the islands. In addition, he had served as a judge of the International Criminal Court (in regard to Yugoslavia and Rwanda) in the Hague.[16] He had adjudicated difficult issues of unspeakable violence. He was an international big shot.

He was also a very gracious man. In only a few moments after the guards had relayed our request to President Carmona, one of the guards approached us, grinning from ear to ear. "The president said that he'd be delighted to meet you. But you'll have to wait here for about fifteen minutes, and then he'll be free to come down and say hello." And the guards ushered us to the side of the long driveway to wait for the president.

Muttering in annoyance at time wasted, one or two couples left our group to continue touring on their own. A third couple left our group.

They didn't believe the distinguished president would really appear, and they didn't want to lose any more time out of their day.

But sure enough, in precisely fifteen minutes, the tall, erect, graying but still handsome president appeared. He was flanked by six well-built and visibly armed guards. They watched him like hawks as he shook hands with each of us, welcoming us individually and as a group to Trinidad. But, other than that initial contact, the body guards didn't let us close enough to touch him.

The role of the president in Trinidad is largely ceremonial. He "reigns" but does not govern. The day-to-day business of the country is done by the prime minister (who would probably have been too busy to see us). President Carmona inquired as to our own nationalities and backgrounds, and then he told us a little about his own. Of African, Amerindian, and Spanish descent, he was the eldest of six children. Born in South Trinidad and well educated, he became a skilled lawyer of considerable repute and eventually progressed to the post of honor he now holds.

Then he began to talk of other things, of his country and the world. About the way people treat one another. He had been very upset, he told us, by some recent murders in Trinidad that had dominated the newspapers, and he assured us that this violence was not characteristic of his country. He talked of the distressing violent behavior that was affecting the entire globe and of the need for peace worldwide. Then he pointed to the uncivil discourse of recent years as a kind of virus infecting the world—and suggested how each of us could affect toxic outcomes by using civil discourse with everyone with whom we come in contact.

"It all begins right here," he told us, "with shaking hands, with getting to know one another, by treating each other politely and humanely." There were almost tears gathering in his eyes, as he shared himself so passionately and honestly with us. He was leading by example. With presidential behavior.

He also knew a photo-op when he saw one. Everyone in our group had their cell phones out by now, recording this special moment. The president's photographers got in plenty of their own shots with more official cameras. Tomorrow's newspapers would have photos of good human relations on their front pages. Later that night, president Carmona also had photos of the best prints delivered to our cruise ship. It was an occasion to be shared—and remembered. Just like in biblical times, we went to see the president, and he just happened to be there.

SECTION FOUR

Panama Canal, Central and South America

Section 4, Panama, Central America
Ancient Mayan ruins in Izapa, Chiapas,
Mexico (bordering Guatemala).
Photo credit: Janet Spiegel©2017

A Green Shoot Grows

*A*few months before I was ordained as a rabbi, I initiated a pluralistic Jewish study group called *Beit Kulam* (House of Togetherness), now entering its sixth year. Held in our living room, it takes the form of a cozy, Sunday morning breakfast club (bagels with cream cheese, delicious home-baked goods, really good coffee, and ample schmoozing time before the sessions start—and even after, as people get to know one another). Some people attend via Skype or Facetime from places like Vancouver, BC, or even Venezuela or Israel. Usually some fifteen to twenty people attend each study session in person, plus several virtual attendees, which is a really good size for vigorous and informed discussion on continuing themes.

Some *Beit Kulam* members are very knowledgeable, well versed in Judaism; others are just beginning to learn what it means to be a Jew. Some of the people who attend are not Jewish but are attracted by the topics, and by the inclusive, homey atmosphere. Everyone is welcome.

Why do they come to *Beit Kulam*? Because we discuss things they want to know or that they feel too shy to ask in a more formal setting—complex ethical or sensitive issues many synagogues just don't have the time or inclination to examine in depth. After my presentation on a particular topic, usually part of a theme extending over several sessions, our *Beit Kulam* attendees engage in vigorous discussion.

* * * *

One of the themes my study group tackled involved exploring what really may have happened to the Ten "Lost" Jewish Tribes. We examined, and looked beyond, some of the theories that have been proposed at different times but since discarded. It was, and is, a fascinating study, which took us through many cultures.

Among the people and places we read and talked about were the ancient Maya, who made their home for centuries in Central America.[17] How could such astonishing mathematical and astrological erudition, as well as architectural abilities, exist in their polytheistic, savage culture? One of the once popular but currently discarded theories is that the Maya were actually the descendants of the ancient Israelites, remnants of a Lost Tribe. The time frame of these theories was a little skewed, however. In fact, the connection may go back earlier, much earlier, all the way to the biblical Tower of Babel.

The Tower of Babel? You're Kidding!

According to mystical Jewish literature (see *Seder Hadorot, Sefer Hayashar, Book of Jubilees*, the *Zohar*,[18] and the *Book of Enoch*[19]), it is entirely possible that there may have been connections between the biblical Israelites and the Maya, but they would have occurred much earlier than the period when the Assyrians conquered and dispersed the Ten Tribes of ancient Northern Israel. In fact, the possible dispersion to Mesoamerica (Central America) may go back to the time of the disgraced builders of the Tower of Babel, as is recounted in the Torah (Genesis 11:1-9).

In this view, God was furious, not because the builders were trying to reach the heavens, but because they were trying to usurp God's power. And so the Torah portrays God as dispersing the people all over the world and confounding their language, so that they now spoke many languages and could no longer understand one another. This scattering of the people likely happened around 1765 BCE. The Mayan civilization is believed to have its origins around 2,000 BCE or earlier, so it is quite possible that at least some of the Tower of Babel people may have been the biblical forebears of the Maya. This is a theory, remember.

Our Genius Ancestor, Enoch…[20]

Here is where our ancestor, Enoch, and his many descendants come into the picture. Who was Enoch? In terms of his ancestry, he was the great-great-grandson of the biblical Seth, a son of Adam. The timeline and intricate genealogy of the Enoch story coincide with the beginnings of Mayan civilization—and of the birth of the Mayan calendar.

In terms of his abilities, Enoch was celebrated for his astounding astronomical and mathematical knowledge and teachings. He understood the course of the planetary bodies. He was skilled in the building of cities. The mystical *Zohar* claimed that Enoch possessed a book containing the inner secrets of wisdom that originated from the Garden of Eden. The Greeks even credited him with the invention of writing.

It is possible that one of Enoch's descendants, who lived during the time of the Tower of Babel, may have settled in the area now called the Yucatan (perhaps in honor of his ancestor, Yoktan). Presumably, Enoch's knowledge was passed to his descendants and through them to the Maya, who integrated this knowledge into their own cyclical calendar.

In fact, the Maya had two calendars, the first a sacred calendar called "the Calendar Round," which was lunar, and the second referred to as "the Long Count Calendar" (these dates were usually found on inscriptions), which was solar based. The Maya reconciled the two calendars. They also created the concept of the zero.

The Calendar Round (52 years)

In *Breaking the Maya Code*, author Michael Coe, a long recognized authority on Mayan culture, explains the 260 days of the sacred Calendar Round as evoking the nine-month period of gestation.[21] This, he says, results from "the never-ending [for more than 2,500 years] permutation of 13 numbers with a rigid sequence of 20 named days [13 x 20 = 260]." But that's not all. As Coe further explains, "[R]un this count against the 365 days of the solar year," and you'll get the 52-year Calendar Round, "the Mesoamerican equivalent of our century."[22] Amazing! If mathematics is your forte, as mine is not, you'll enjoy figuring this out.

What about the second Mayan calendar, usually referred to as "The Long Count Calendar"?

The Long Count Calendar

This second Mayan calendar appeared near the end of the Mayan Pre-Classic period (the last century BCE). To quote Michael Coe once again, "Unlike dates in the Calendar Round, which are fixed only within a never ending [recurring] cycle of 52 years ... Long Count dates are given in a day-to-day count, which began in the year 3114 BC."[23]

In recent times, there were dire predictions about what would happen when the revered Mayan calendar ended its 5,000 year cycle.[24] In fact, frightened people all over the globe believed that the world would end in 2012 AD, when the calendar concluded.

Nevertheless, the physical world of those long ago Maya—and the rest of the planet with it—did not end in December 2012. No, the globe did not erupt in chaos because, in Mayan culture, when you come to the end of a cycle, it simply starts all over again. The new cycle represents an era of regeneration and hope for the future. That, too, is the story recounted throughout the Hebrew Bible.

> *"But a shoot shall grow out of the stump of Jesse,*
> *A twig shall sprout from his stock"* (Isaiah 11:1-2).[25]

Even if the tree is felled, a green shoot will eventually grow from the stump. Even if it takes thousands of years.

The Peacock's Tale

*L*ittle did I know as our *Beit Kulam* group speculated about the Maya that I would soon find myself in Guatemala, the birthplace of the Mayan calendar. Once again, I had happily agreed to serve as rabbi on another trip to far-away lands, this time to Central America. After clearing the Panama Canal, our first port of call was in Columbia, which is actually South America.

For years I had a busy writing and editing service. Among the books, articles, speeches, and what-have-you that I edited, there were usually two or three master's or doctoral theses every year. And I learned a great deal from them. One thesis that I found particularly spiritually attractive concerned equine therapy,[26] something that has since proven very successful, especially with teenagers, but at that time it was still regarded with considerable skepticism, particularly by this graduate student's professor. The student ended up dedicating her remarkable thesis to her horse and to me.

One of the interesting things I learned from her thesis was that in animal life there are two categories: predators and prey. Apparently, predators have eyes placed to look straight in front of them, so that they can spot prey quickly. Prey, on the other hand, have eyes placed on the side of their heads so that they can see the predators coming more easily and run away. Prey always have a nervous quality, a marked sensitivity to their surroundings.

And so now I come to the peacock's tail. I've been thinking about that spunky peacock and his protective tail feathers ever since I returned from Central America to sunny California, safe and sound. Once our ship completed its nine-hour trip through the historic Panama Canal, moving into open waters, we had been under the protection of the US coastguard (manning mounted guns), with a sister cruise ship closely following. I thought briefly about pirates, terrorists, then banished these fears. Together we were a BIG SHAPE— spread out like a preening peacock's tail feathers—as we traveled, and I, for one, was glad to proceed in this close, sea-borne caravan until we reached Columbia.

Over the years, I have seen peacocks in various places, zoos mostly, or animal parks that let them roam to a degree. But never one like this peacock. I spotted him in the National Aviary Park in Cartagena among all the other beautiful birds of many colors. I have since learned that the peacock was originally an East Indian bird, but I cannot imagine a bird's colors being more vibrant, his tail feathers so long anywhere else but in Cartagena. As they shone in the sun, the sight was enough to make you "get religion," to stir your wonder of the Cosmos and its creator.

This peacock roamed around freely within the area covered by the Columbian Aviary's high, gauzy ceiling, looking humans in the eyes curiously, without fear, having learned already that at least in this protected setting, the people making contact with him were not a danger to him. Even though peacocks can bite quite fiercely if they sense they will be harmed, even though this peacock's eyes were on the side of the head, he knew he was not at risk here. It was a safe space. My green eyes and his black eyes continued a silent conversation for quite a while, as he cocked his head from side to side, assessing me. Is this a good human being?

Then the next day the ship transporting me along with 2,000 other passengers and 1,000 crew, stopped in Costa Rica. We had returned to Central America, which is actually part of North America. Here those of us who chose to explore a mangrove swamp—similar swamps may be found where a river meets the sea—boarded a small boat. We travelled slowly through the narrow, brownish, swampy waters. On the shores on either side of the mangrove swamp, we could spot—often with difficulty because they were so well camouflaged—some of the bird species that we had seen in the Columbian aviary. But here in Costa Rica, they were in their natural setting. So were very scary crocodiles, predators who waited, in the swamp, just their eyes and nostrils peering above the water, for foolish prey to come too close. (Actually, crocs can run pretty fast on land—not a good idea to encounter them there either!)

And then I spotted the peacock on the shore. Not the same peacock that I had seen in Columbia, of course, but equally beautiful, strutting around with his tail feathers glowing with iridescent colors, shining in the sun. Like the Columbian peacock, the Costa Rican peacock evoked a sense of wonder in me, a connection to Creation. How could a living creature on the shore of a swamp be so beautiful? Meanwhile his six peacock wives, dowdy brown and white hens, without long tail feathers gifted by an artistic God, fed on the plant life. One might say charitably that they were dressed modestly.

Once the gorgeous peacock spotted the crocodile, he went into defense mode. How? He didn't run; he didn't freeze. He stood his ground. He approached the shore as closely as he dared, turned around, and raised his tail feathers. Generally speaking, when a peacock spreads his tail feathers, a casual observer may think that he is preening. But when a peacock turns around and spreads his tail feathers in defense, his backside is a dowdy brown and white, just like the hens that he is protecting—and, come to think of it, close to the color of that low-lying crocodile. Not only are these dull feathers a camouflage, but spread out like that as the peacock presents his behind to the enemy, they make a REALLY BIG SHAPE. Enough to keep that predator croc in the water. The croc doesn't want to mess with that scary shape, even though, when you take a second look, it's balanced on spindly, prey-like, peacock legs.

What's really scary, it seems to me, whether it's a croc in a mangrove swamp or a human being in our more usual habitats, is that so often it's hard to tell the predator from the prey. After all, human beings have eyes on the front of their faces, not the sides.

Can prey become predators? Or vice versa. There's that troubling question! Can human predators be disguised by the direction of their eyes? What if they hide their intentions with sunglasses? Does concern for others—loving-kindness, connectedness—infuse their vision, change that direction? Or does too much concern have the propensity to turn us, defenseless, into unwitting prey? How do we find a balance between predator and prey, both at home and in distant lands?

This was a theme that continued to intrigue me as we toured Central America.

The Ring of Fire

Still protected by the US Coast Guard, we approached the boundaries of our next port of call. It was springtime in Guatemala. I am so grateful to the ship's lecturers, the slides or films shown, the guides, the reading material that helped me understand the complex history, much of it lost, of this remarkable place.

I already knew, as I wrote in the previous stories, that long ago, Guatemala was the home of the remarkable Mayan culture, the birthplace of its creation story and its two calendars (one lunar, one solar, which they intercalated); of remarkable astronomical calculations; of the complex cycle of its culture; of a written language whose mysterious code has been cracked, if not fully understood, in modern times. Their culture was also the inspiration of powerful artistic representations based on the natural world, on the animals around them, like the jaguar, whose speed and cunning strength they venerated. Or the Maize God, the super-god that gave them food.

Yet, here in this place thinly covered with limestone and volcanic ash where food was—and is—so hard to grow, an unalterable fact was embedded in their culture. The Maya knew they were, above all and without warning, the prey of the all-consuming mountains, and so, for centuries, they tried to propitiate the gods of the volcanos by feeding them human sacrifices. Many of these sacrificed humans were captives taken from other tribes with whom the Maya were warring.

As I stood there, an awestruck visitor to this land in the twenty-first century, misty clouds floated just below the summits of the twenty-three volcanos ringing the country, creating an other-worldly quality.

Mystical, like the ancient literature that connected the biblical Enoch with this part of Central America.

Most of these volcanos are still active or dormant. When fiery lava still flows down their sides, when the volcanos erupt at times, killing everything in their wake, is the spiritual legend of the ancient Maya who once fed them human bodies still predatory in nature? Has it been redeemed by time—and dispersion? Once again I questioned the balance between predator and prey. Is it ever shifting, that balance? Can one, at different times, be both predator and prey?

The atmosphere as I continued to gaze at the distant volcanos was surreal. With every passing moment, I become more and more aware of my own mortality. Softly I hummed the melody of the *Una Tana Tokef*, the sacred prayer Jews recite at Rosh Hashana, the Jewish New Year: "Who shall live and who shall die?" These words capturing the deepest insights of the Jewish relationship to the divine are also applicable to the reality of this Central American country still troubled by violence and death.

The Maya are long gone—although some remnants of that ancient people, now melded with Mexican culture, still profess to derive from that civilization. Our 21st century mathematicians still marvel at the complex astronomical knowledge of a proud people who sacrificed individuals to propitiate the fierce deities they invented to explain the volcanic eruptions. At the very same time they were exhibiting advanced mathematical knowledge and building complex structures, not to mention growing abundant crops on the land, the prosperous Maya were tearing out human hearts on the sacrificial altars of their religious cult.

Today recovered Mayan artwork in museums reveals the armed predator with his foot on the neck of his human prey. Depending on circumstances, it seems, prey and predator were interchangeable. Can people capable of impressive abstract thought literally remove the heart from a live person—in order to ingest that person's power—on a sacrificial altar and still remain spiritual human beings? Or do they then become indistinguishable from the wild animal life that inhabits their landscape? Do they become a human landscape informed by the fury of the volcanos? Do they transcend their animal selves to become artists who depict the life of that time in ways that continue to touch the heart of those who view their work in later centuries?

* * * *

The artistic side of Guatemalan life was revealed in an especially complimentary way when we visited the Casa Santo Domingo in Antigua (the old capital of Guatemala, itself once reduced to ruins in an earthquake and subsequently restored). The Casa consists of three museums featuring different aspects of Guatemalan culture and combined in an aesthetically-conceived complex, presided over by Dominican monks. For me, the most striking exhibit was a large display featuring ancient Mayan sculpture. Each sculpture of antiquity was accompanied by exquisite modern day sculptures (lent to the exhibit from galleries around the world) with the same themes—themes common to every culture in every generation: the elements, nature, motherhood, love, grief. My daughter and I spent the entire day at this extraordinary Casa, itself surrounded by beautiful gardens. We drank wine, though, at the excellent restaurant because Guatemalan water is advisedly not for tourists who have not yet developed sufficient local microbes in their systems to avert intestinal disaster.

We also felt physically secure inside this complex because, in addition to the violent ramifications of the dangerous drug cartels and gang violence the population feared, Guatemalan borders were being besieged by desperate Venezuelan refugees seeking to flee the multiple disasters of their own corrupt country—including armed conflict at the border.

Real Estate on Mars?

Why did the ancient Maya leave? Although there are many theories, no one really knows why. Did an especially disastrous earthquake or volcanic eruption occur, destroying everything in its wake? Did the earth grow less fertile, the crops fail, so that they relocated? Were they carried away into outer space by aliens?

Apparently, while the upper classes of Mayan culture disappeared, the lower working classes remained. Similarly, when the ancient Jews were carried off to exile in Babylonia, only the upper echelon of society and the priests were "taken;" the "people" were left to fend for themselves.

Perhaps it was climate change. Like similar periods that have been captured in the Hebrew Bible, long years of drought with resulting famine caused the Maya to leave. Perhaps there was nothing to eat. Slowly, the wild animals, both prey and predator, disappeared, and eventually the remaining Maya left for other places. Most assimilated into Mexico.

Along with the Guatemalan borders that spill into Mexico, there are still vestiges of the Mayan culture today. It was in adjacent Mexico that I stood in the very field—actually a games-playing site: a ball field—that marked the birthplace of the long-lost Mayan civilization. Considerable additional architectural excavation could be done on the bordering fields if not for the fact that they are now private property. They belong to people who have built their houses and businesses there. No way they want them excavated.

However, from the ball court, we could get the general idea of the vast Mayan culture that was. We could still look into the distance and see the ring of fire—the volcanos—presenting a misted but ever-present danger. To this day, recurrent volcanic eruptions result in earthquakes and other natural disasters that wreak their vengeance on a population already suffering from a continuing cycle of poverty.

Over-population on a scale we do not know in the US or Canada is a huge problem in Central America and in other parts of the world that I have visited. In Central America, one reason is a lack of education about family planning. A second reason is the religious stigma of using birth control in a now mainly Catholic country. Thirdly, the governments do not have the resources to cope with the needs of their own populations, let alone the re-settling problems that so many new people, leaving even worse situations, bring in their wake. Their governments can't handle it, and gangsters run their countries.

When human-inflicted evils, like the current mayhem of drug cartels and vicious gangs, are added to this mix, those who can, flee. If you live here, you would do well to be God-fearing.

* * * *

As I sat comfortably on a bus on my trip through the modern day Mexico landscape bordering Guatemala, the poverty of the surrounding countryside was evident until we approached a small city in the southern Mexican state of Chiapas. Here, where Mayan artifacts dot the countryside, huge efforts were being made by the population to upgrade their way of life.

We stopped at a brand new cultural and educational center, of which the local people were obviously extremely proud. We tourists were first treated not only to traditional dancing and singing, but to some modern compositions as well. Then we were offered a tour of the city's newest educational accomplishment. It featured, not unsurprisingly—astronomy being indigenous to the Maya—a striking, very modern planetarium and a theater, both created with ingenuity and artistry. The ceilings of the planetarium were alive with lighted, vibrantly colored astrological signs that featured the signature animals, like the jaguar, of the Mayan culture.

Maybe the Maya of old knew what they were doing when they studied the planetary universe with astrological knowledge astonishing for their time. We earthlings may need the resources of some of those planets sooner than we think.

Anyone selling real estate on Mars?

Getting the Balance Right

*W*hen I was an "Honors English" undergraduate student at McGill University so many years ago, my concentration was mainly on theater and drama, along, of course, with literature. History, too. I still remember how upset I was to learn about Antonin Artaud's "Theatre of Cruelty."[27] It was indeed a cruel message for me to absorb, a young girl who had entered university at sixteen years of age, and who believed that, ideally, the role of the arts was to convey not only life's beauty—and yes, its vagaries and sorrows—but also to inspire, and, in so doing, to reach for the essence of the divine. I didn't know when I was a teenager that one day, much later in life, I would become a rabbi.

Who was Antonin Artaud (1896-1948)?

His then *avant-guarde* argument, a dramatic one indeed, was that nature is cruel, the ultimate cruelty, and that no matter what human beings build or create, no matter how much they think they have conquered the desert, the jungle, or the sea, no matter what great civilizations they build, nature will persevere in the end. Just as *Kohelet* postulates in the Hebrew Bible, (Ecclesiastes 1:2), everything is *ephemeral* (a better English translation of the Hebrew word "*hevel*" than "vanity.") That is what Artaud's plays purported to show: Eventually, it is only a matter of time, nature reclaims it. Like sand castles washed away by the tide, as we discover in childhood, to fragmented Torah texts or pottery shards or valuables secreted in tombs, or even whole cities unearthed centuries later, we learn that nature takes back by what is later revealed.

Artaud's theories seemed quite credible to me when terrifying earthquakes raged in Hawaii (which became the fiftieth US state on August 21, 1959). Whenever earthquakes erupt, it is easy to understand why the original inhabitants of the Hawaiian Islands invented a goddess named Pele who needed to be propitiated so that she would not erupt.

My children and I walked on those same black lava beds when we visited Big Island in the early 1980s, so the videos and oral reports of Kilauea's major eruption in 1986 seem almost beyond belief to me. True, red embers were visible through the fissures even when we visited, and we were permitted to stay only a few minutes because of the sulfur gas constantly emitted. However, the capable rangers and knowledgeable geologists had it all under control then. Each day they checked their up-to-the-minute scientific information and reconfigured where it was safe for tourists to be. When two of my children strayed too long, however, their throats were very sore the next day. In recent years, access has been much more limited, I am told.

As if in response to Kilauea's continuing fury over the years, echoing volcanic disasters have erupted in other areas of the world. In Guatemala, surrounded by "the ring of fire" of its enveloping mountains, volcanic fury has been raging repeatedly. When I visited there, I was enthralled by the fact that this land, these mountains cloaked in mist just beneath their summits, represent the birthplace of the almost lost Mayan culture. But why do people stay now? Why do people choose to live near volcanos—near Pompei, for example, in Italy, or in Santorini in Greece? Perhaps it's because inspiration couples with the possibility of destruction there. Perhaps it's because somehow, in the enormity of what has happened, what can still happen with blinding speed, it feels close to God.

As I watched film clips of natural disaster raging in Hawaii (the last major eruption occurred on May 3, 2018), I remembered sitting in the mystical vortex between two crystal-embedded mountains there and hearing the mountains echo with sound, like giant radios. What were they transmitting? What messages have they still to convey?

And I remembered walking (a little apprehensively, I admit) two decades earlier through the long lava tube that cut right through the Kilauea volcano. Remarkably, nature had made it into a beautiful rain forest, filled with green plants and gorgeous flowers—right there in the middle of the volcano. The rain forest had all the natural ingredients it needed to flourish.

In God's world, creation coexists with destruction. Our task, as God's partners in creation, is to get the balance right.

SECTION FIVE

The Mediterranean

Section 5, Mediterranean
Commonly used door knocker representing *Hamza* (hand of God or hand of Miriam in Judaism) or *Fatimah's hand* (in Islam) on old building in Rhodes, Greece.
Photo credit: Janet Spiegel©2016

Seeking Jewish Life in Spain?

500 Years Ago

*D*espite the fact that the Spanish government, a democratic monarchy now headed by King Juan Carlos' son, Felipe VI, has tried to redeem the ugly facts of the long ago expulsion of Spain's Jews, the facts remain. It happened 500 years ago. Amazingly, in 2014, the well-meaning Spanish government decided to offer full citizenship to Jews whose ancestors were once expelled from Spain. Better late than never. Yet, despite this enticement to come back, the number of Jews living in Spain still remains small.

As history reminds us, the Jewish presence in Spain effectively ended with the decision of the devoutly Catholic monarchs of Spain, Queen Isabella and King Ferdinand, to establish what was known as the Spanish Inquisition in 1478. Officially it was called "The Tribunal of the Holy Office of the Inquisition." There were to be no heretics in Spain.

Some fifteen years later, The Edict of Expulsion, issued in 1492, compelled all Jews, rich or poor, either to convert or to leave the country within a four-month window.[28] There were some 300,000 Jews in Spain! Many of their families not only had been living in Spain for centuries but had also contributed largely to the country's brilliance and prosperity. Of these, 40,000 to 100,000 (estimates vary) Jews refused to convert. Consequently, they were forced to liquidate everything they owned—if indeed they could—and flee.

The majority of the Spanish Jews, however, wished to remain in Spain; in order to do so, they were forced to convert to Catholicism.

Forever after, they were known as *Conversos* (or derogatively, *Marranos*, meaning pigs). Although many *Conversos* adhered to Judaism in secret, it was a dangerous practice. They were constantly suspected of "Judaizing." Discovery of secret practice or Jewish associations incurred severe punishments, such as torture or burning at the stake. Confiscated holy books were burned. Assets were seized.

Despite the efforts of a prominent, wealthy, Jewish scholar and businessman, Don Isaac Abravanel—who reportedly had financed the three ships for Columbus' voyage to the New World (the Nina, the Pinta, and the Santa Maria) in order to influence the rulers to delay or rescind this order—the rulers remained firm. They were under the indomitable sway of the Grand Inquisitor, Torquemada. No Jews in Spain. In addition, it was undoubtedly to the rulers' economic advantage to seize Jewish properties and other valuable assets that could not be transacted within the four-month deadline.

Many Spanish Jews fled in terror to nearby Portugal (where, unfortunately, their safety was very brief) and to the other countries of the Mediterranean. Others fled across the Mediterranean to Arab lands. They carried their culture, their Spanish language, and their haunting Ladino songs with them. Some also carried the keys to the old synagogues and passed them down. Always, these *Sephardim* hoped to return. For the first time in centuries, they can.

A Period of Transition: 1975

The first time I visited Spain was in 1975. It was a period of transition from the dictatorship of General Francisco Franco, which had begun in 1939 after he led his right-wing Nationalist party to victory in the fiercely fought Spanish Civil War. During World War II, Spain leaned toward the Nazis in Germany and the Fascists in Italy.

By 1975, when Franco died and the dictatorship ended, local people still seemed guarded, reluctant to converse with foreigners. Policemen helmeted in the curious Spanish manner were still evident on the streets of Barcelona, Catalonia—the first city in southern Spain on my tour's itinerary. While the beautiful Costa del Sol was being developed as a resort area, stalled projects, reflecting the political uncertainty, could be seen along the beaches. The whole country, it seemed, had warily assumed a waiting posture as the process of establishing a democracy had begun under a monarch, King Juan Carlos, as head of State.

The Spain I was revisiting four decades later, accompanied this time by my daughter Janet, was a happy, bustling place.[29] People had welcoming smiles for visitors and, in Barcelona, there was great pride in the extravagantly joyful, out-of-the-box Gaudi architecture that is the pride of this lovely city; the icing on the cake is that there are beautiful beaches too.

Barcelona, however, has a noticeable paucity of Jews. According to the *Jewish Virtual Library*, about 5,000 live in Barcelona now, while some 12,000 Jews live in Madrid (the Conservative *Beit El* synagogue is there), Malaga, and Barcelona combined.[30] There is a small synagogue converted to a museum in Toledo. However, depending on the source, estimates for Jews living in Spain today vary considerably, anywhere from 13,000 to 50,000. A handful of Jews live in Valencia and Marbella, as well as in two North African enclaves. Once there were so many more.

Back in Los Angeles, I had researched the old Jewish synagogue still standing in the center of Barcelona. Its name, *Sinagoga Major de Barcelona*, suggests its past importance. Dating back to the sixth century CE, with sturdy Roman foundations and the remains of arched Roman walls, it may well be the oldest synagogue in Europe. In fact, it is one of only five medieval synagogues that have survived. Its two rooms—that's it!—are pictured on the Internet.[31] Since I had already viewed the photographs, the *Sinagoga's* rooms seemed familiar when I arrived in person, except that they seemed so much smaller than I had anticipated. In order to enter, I had to descend a flight of stairs. Because of its great age and the fact that it had been unearthed, the little synagogue was very considerably lower in the ground than the surrounding buildings.

I had the sense of entering a dimly-lit cave. That's what it felt like—a smallish cave with a structure held up by enduring Roman walls. Two ladies (Jewish?) sat there in folding chairs, ready to impart information to visitors. They told us that there was probably a *mikveh* buried under the adjoining building, but it could not be excavated because it was the private property of other people (who understandably didn't want their café dug up).

Given the good will of the current Spanish government, the efforts to rebuild Jewish life in Spain continue. There is also, however, a strong and very disturbing anti-Israel, pro-Palestinian feeling pervading the country—a new kind of antisemitism, even though few Spanish people have ever met an actual Jew. Or even have a true understanding of what happened to the Jews in Spain 500 years ago.[32]

Unfortunately, what passes for the old Jewish quarter in Barcelona is really a figment of the imagination. It's not even a good stage set. In reality, it consists of a bunch of engraved plaques attached to tall brick buildings constructed long after the original buildings were demolished. The plaques identify where the original buildings in the narrow alleys of the Jewish quarter ONCE stood. None of the brick buildings were the original buildings. Consequently, our visit there was a disappointment.

Until. One of the walls of a building—using stones harvested from the site of the quarter's long ago cemetery—had individual names in Hebrew letters etched in them. What??? Salvaged stones from the old Jewish cemetery had been built into the new wall. I kissed the Hebrew names etched in each marked stone within my reach. Even centuries later, those who visit this quarter-that-isn't can still honor the Jews who once were there.

Even though, as Daniella Levy writes in her excellent article about her own, more extensive visit to Spain,[33] she found a pro-Palestinian slogan (*Palestina Libra*)— scrawled maliciously across the Hebrew letters identifying the site of the old Jewish quarter.

As I wrote in the guest book of the *Sinagoga Major*, "I am still here."

A Shofar Sounds in Venice!

From the harbor where we disembarked, my daughter and I had walked almost the length of the Venetian canal to reach the Old Jewish Quarter. By contrast to the location of the Old Jewish Quarter in Spain, in Venice it was restored, vibrant, and alive with the sound of young, black-clad and hatted *Chabad* [34](a modern day Hasidic movement that preaches its religious philosophy around the world) students showing interested male tourists how to lay *tefillin* (little leather cubes containing scriptural passages; fastened to the head and arm by leather straps, they are used for prayerful morning meditation)—and how to blow the *shofar* (a ram's horn traditionally used to herald the Jewish New Year). Scattered on a long table were *shofarot* (plural of *shofar*, horns) of various shapes and sizes. In preparation for my rabbinic engagement on this Mediterranean cruise over the High Holy Days, I had carefully packed a small, whitish, bubble-wrapped, Israeli ram's horn—chosen over my black Yemenite antelope's horn, curlier and harder to fit in the suitcase. I didn't know that I would be able to find a *shofar*—from such a plentiful array—in the Village Square of the Old Jewish quarter in Venice. You have to hand it to Chabad (even if they don't accept women rabbis yet!).

The long table was set out in front of a storefront synagogue, a comfortable prayer space for travelers that Chabad had set up, and right next to it was—yes, a small kosher restaurant. Both were full. *Klezmer* music played, and it was next to impossible to keep my feet from dancing. The joyful atmosphere was infectious. It was old Jewish Venice revived.

In the Judaica shop, I was drawn to and almost purchased a good-sized Torah scroll (available in a smaller size, too, but harder to read) that featured a continuous, brightly-colored comic strip to tell the story of the Five Books of Moses. The balloons emanating from the characters in the story were in English (other vernacular languages may have been available), and bannered directly above each comic strip was the Hebrew text. It was a beautiful creation, not garish at all, not sacrilegious. A good teaching tool to interest *Bar/Bat Mitzvah* candidates, I thought. And I'm not one to be thrilled by comic books (even though I did devour *Wonder Woman* comics and plenty of others when I was a kid).

"How much?" I asked the kind-faced Hasidic man (a member of a Jewish spiritual movement emphasizing little acts of kindness and love over often unattainable perfection in religious practice; led by the Baal Shem Tov in the eighteenth century, Hasidism quickly spread from Western Ukraine through Eastern Europe). That's when I found out that the price was $1,000. That's why there were donation pages preceding the text to record the names of the givers. Probably the scroll was intended as a *Bar/Bat Mitzvah* gift. I still wavered—it was so unusual. Where would I ever find such a scroll again?

In Florida, that's where! The truly inspired artist lives in the US, and the scrolls were produced there, too. "It takes her a year to make each scroll," the Hasidic man said gently. He was a great salesman, but now he wanted to close the sale. The Judaica shop would ship it to Los Angeles for me, but the price was the price.

"Hmmm," I prevaricated. Buying it would decimate my shopping budget for the entire, three-week trip. "I think we'll take some time to think about it. We want to visit the restored synagogue first."

So my daughter and I climbed the steps to the moderately-sized, Sephardic synagogue on an upper floor overlooking the square and listened to an informative guide explain its history, and how it had, like everything else in the quarter, been so lovingly restored.

Then we returned to the Judaica store where I regretfully told the Hasidic man, whose eyes still smiled at us, that we couldn't afford the comic book Torah, but the Hanukah *dreidels* (miniature tops that spin and are used for a children's game) were also compelling. So we settled for several really beautiful *dreidels* crafted in Murano glass.

I haven't been to Florida in years, but the next time I visit there, I'll look up the inspired artist who creates special Torahs for *Bar* and *Bat Mitzvah* kids.

Blow With All Your Heart!

*D*id I tell you that I can't blow the *shofar*? I have tried and tried. But I'm a rabbi who can't even blow up a balloon without getting winded. I could excuse myself by saying, "Oh well, that's what happens when you're well into your eighties." Instead I keep trying.

So first I bought a small one, direct from Israel, a ram's horn with a kosher sticker (it's still in place on the horn). And then I tried and tried to blow it. Not a sound. Over and over again on many occasions, I have tried to produce at least a little noise with my *shofar*. *Nada*, as we say in California. Nothing.

At this point, it's only rational—right?—to think that the fault was not with my blowing ability but rather with the *shofar*. What kind of a kosher *shofar* was this short, white horn, sticker and all? That's when I went shopping and bought a pretty, ebony black, Yemenite *shofar*. Also kosher, very curvy, and from Israel as well, it came from an antelope, not a ram. It's skinnier than the ram's horn, like a *shofar* that's been trying to lose weight. "Aha!" I thought. "This looks like a *shofar* made for me,' and, without a second thought, I bought it.

Sadly, I couldn't produce a single sound from it. Not one, even though I tried to blow the *shofar* many different ways. This couldn't be a coincidence. Why couldn't I get ANY *shofar* to sound for me?

Just then, my then sixteen-year-old granddaughter, entered the room and saw me huffing and puffing, almost in tears. "What's wrong, Grandma?" she asked, concerned. "Can you get any kind of noise from this *shofar*?" I asked her. "It's from an antelope in Yemen." She took the *shofar* from my hands, put it to her mouth, and drew from it a long, soulful, teenage blast.

"Sure," she said. "It's easy." I took the ram's horn from its place in the cabinet. "How about this one?" She put it to her lips, and again drew from it a deeper sound than the first one. "No sweat," she said. "It's easy."

So it wasn't the fault of the antelope, not the fault of the sheep, or the people who put stickers on.

My other granddaughter, then a newly-minted thirteen, heard all the noise and came running into the room. "Here," I said, handing her one of the *shofarot*. "Can you blow these?" She gave me a reproving look. "Grandma, I've already had my *bat mitzvah*!" On the first try, she blew strong, firm blasts from the *shofar* she selected. And then from the other one. The blasts were so loud, they sounded like a ship's horn making its way through the fog. Or maybe a *shofar*—ram's horn, antelope's horn, straight, curly, it doesn't matter—sounding exactly the way it was supposed to. You could hear it from a mountain top.

* * * *

The fact remained that my granddaughters with powerful lungs and musical ability were not coming with me on my High Holy Day assignment on a cruise ship. And now I knew that there was nothing wrong with either of my *shofarot*. Well, on a cruise ship you have to improvise. Maybe I would find someone who could play the trumpet on the ship, or at least a wind instrument. So when my little "congregation-at-sea" assembled on the Sabbath prior to Rosh Hashana, the Jewish New Year, I asked if, by chance, anyone could play the *shofar* or a wind instrument.

To my surprise, a lively, middle-aged man spoke up. "I can play the trumpet," he offered.

Of course I was delighted. I explained that our trumpet would be a *shofar*, if he could blow that too. The ancient sound of the *shofar* is like the trumpet-blasts acknowledging the coronation of a sovereign—the Sovereign of the World—God.

"I'll try," he said. "My name's John."

While I couldn't produce a sound from the *shofar* myself, I did know the pattern of sounds that the *shofar* should produce for the High Holy Days. So the two of us spent an afternoon in the nightclub on the top level of the ship; normally, it wasn't used during the day, and we were able to fill its quiet with lots of *shofar* noise, while John got used to the sound patterns this *shofar* could ably produce. During the actual service I, as the rabbi, would call out the Hebrew words meant to evoke the pattern of sounds that John would draw forth from the *shofar*. The *shofar's* sounds stir our conscience, individually and collectively, to confront our past mistakes.

Tkiyah Shevarim Truah Tkiyah
Tkiyah Shevarim Truah Tkiyah
Tkiyah Shevarim Truah Tkiyah[35]

As we practiced the sounds together—word call and musical response, I could see that John was moved almost to tears.

"If we miss the mark, we can always try again," I told John. And he blew his practice notes of the *Tkiyah Gedola*, the final long, long blast of the *Great Shofar* until he was so red in the face, he looked like he would burst—with joy, I thought.

During that meaningful afternoon, John poured out his heart to me. He was not actually a Jew. Although he had been born a Christian, he had always felt drawn to Judaism. Eventually, he had become a Jew for Jesus, a Messianic Jew.

We talked for a long time. John was a deeply soulful person who had read widely. He had a highly developed brain that interpreted the world mathematically and was attracted to Gematria. On his own, he had studied and had an appreciation of many of the mystical precepts of Kabbala (not the red string kind!), but he was in spiritual turmoil. He longed to be accepted by the Jewish community.

"You need to study with a rabbi, John," I said. "Jews believe in one God. If you say that you are a Messianic Jew, that means you accept Jesus as divine. You have to decide, and I think you need some help to do that."

We spent a couple of hours on another afternoon addressing some of the issues that concerned him, and the differences between Judaism and Messianism. I made some further suggestions as to whom he could contact for further study, and what readings would help him in his spiritual quest.

"Take your time," I counseled. "In order to become a Jew," as he now claimed he wanted to do, "you would have to convert, and to give up the divinity of Jesus, your belief in him as the Messiah. To become Jewish is a serious commitment. You will have to think about it long and hard."

When it came time for the *Rosh Hashana* services, I was a little uneasy. In order to blow the *shofar* at services, you are really supposed to be a Jew. "I want to become a Jew," he told me before the service. "I'm sure of it," he added with sincerity.

"Time will tell," I replied. "When you blow the *shofar* tonight and tomorrow, John, I want you to blow with all your heart. I want you to blow for the Messiah to come. Our world is in turmoil and surely needs one. It won't matter if he—or she—is coming for the first or second time. Blow for peace in the world."

John smiled. And when he blew the *shofar*, not only did his face get red, but tears of happiness shone in his eyes. It turned out to be a terrific Rosh Hashanah.

At Home with Mersad Berber in Croatia

When we stopped in Croatia, my feelings were mixed about disembarking. It had once been the scene of horrors committed against its Jewish residents before and during World War II. "The Jewish community in Yugoslavia was destroyed during the Second World War. Most synagogues were partially or completely demolished; and synagogues that were not destroyed were plundered, so that they no longer served their purpose," wrote Milica Mihailovic, author of *Judaica in Yugoslavia*.[36] Many of the barbaric acts were committed at the hands of the revolutionary *Ustashis*, Croatian fascists who outdid the Nazis in their zeal, and many thousands of Jews, as well as Serbs and Roma, were slaughtered mercilessly. Recalling that history, I could not help but shudder.

However, the uninterrupted settlement of Jews in these parts actually began long before World War II, starting with the early sixteenth century:

> "Having been expelled by the Inquisition in 1492, the *Sephardim* (Spanish and Portuguese Jews) arrived from Spain and Portugal via Turkey, Greece, and Bulgaria to settle in the territory of present-day Macedonia, Serbia, and Bosnia. *Ashkenazim* came from the North; in particular from Germany, Poland, and Austro-Hungary.... at the end of the eighteenth and during the nineteenth century." [37]

Many of the Ashkenazi Jews settled in areas like Croatia or Voivodina or Slavonia. "The [huge] artistic tradition and creativity developed by Jews in these towns is hard to quantify," wrote Mihailovic, formerly the curator of the Jewish Museum in Belgrade.[38]

After the collapse of Austria-Hungary at the end of World War I in 1918, the Kingdom of Serbs, Croats, and Slovenes was created. Later, in 1929, it was to become Yugoslavia, a country sub-divided into multiple areas within its larger boundaries. Then came the World War II conflict.

Many years have passed since that devastating war ended. However, in the 1990s, an accelerating and bitter conflict ensued between the Croats and the Serbs (with the Bosnians caught in the middle), and finally, Yugoslavia became "the former Yugoslavia," separated into two very different countries: Serbia (which was mainly Muslim) and Croatia (which was not). Dubrovnik, where my daughter and I disembarked, is now a tourist magnet situated in the Adriatic Sea on Croatia's Dalmatian Coast.

Where our ship was moored (along with five other cruise ships, whose thousands of passengers speedily descended upon the historic city) is utterly beautiful. Dubrovnik is an elegant city, with cobblestone roads and graceful buildings that look as if they could be finely-drawn illustrations in history books. For a city with so many visitors, Dubrovnik is remarkably clean. And classy. As we arrived, an orchestra was playing classical music in the main square. We listened to the music for half an hour or so in a fancy outdoor restaurant, along with a saucer of ice cream and pretty little biscuits. This arrangement afforded us comfortable chairs and, thankfully, access to a bathroom up only one flight of stairs.

Quite by chance, I noticed a nearby poster publicizing an art exhibit by Mersad Berber, a Bosnian artist of international, post-classical fame. His work is renowned throughout Europe, although less known in North America. Several of his mystical, multi-media paintings (with gilt paint judiciously applied in the manner of Austrian painter, Gustav Klimt) hang in our living room today. As an artist, Berber, a Muslim, was attracted to both horses and portraits of beautiful women, and his works have an old-world look, as if they had been created centuries ago—and they are gorgeous. His paintings and huge prints are sought after and costly today.

It was quite a walk to get to the art gallery where the Berber paintings were being exhibited, but when we arrived, we were told that the exhibition had ended the day before. We were so disappointed that the gallery owner invited us in. The exhibition had not been taken down yet, she said, and we could take as long as we liked to view the art. And that is how we spent an ecstatic couple of hours with two floors of Berber's works still hanging on the walls.

Why was I so excited about finding the work of this Bosnian artist in Dubrovnik—aside from the fact that I had parted with considerable money to own a few pieces many years earlier? Since Berber died in 2012, the availability of his paintings will decrease and therefore likely increase in price over time, but I had bought a few previously, not as an investor, but because I loved them, and especially because of my long involvement with an exhibition of Jewish art treasures from Yugoslavia some thirty years ago (see "Appendix" for more details).

* * * *

In Dubrovnik, three decades after that long ago exhibition, Janet and I were not only exhilarated from our visit to the art gallery featuring the works of Mersad Berber, we were hungry. There were so many visitors in the city, and the restaurants seemed crowded. And then, again by chance, we literally bumped into a young women, and as we excused ourselves to one another, she told us that she was from Canada. She had come to Dubrovnik to help her widowed mother maintain a small inn and restaurant. Her plan was to stay in Croatia, in Dubrovnik, and try to make a living for her family there.

Yes, their little restaurant was right there on the side street—and they served great food at great prices.

"You won't do better anywhere in the city," she told us with great pride as she led us up a rather steep road to her family's restaurant.

She was right. The street was quiet; the food was great; the price was reasonable; and the climb to get there was worth it. When we invited her to join us, she told us all about life in Dubrovnik, from both a Canadian and a Croatian point of view. Economically, it was harder than in Canada, but satisfying. And she was with family.

We didn't manage to fit in a trip to one of the Croatian beaches, which we heard were delightful, but it could not have been a more rewarding day. Atmosphere, music, art, good food. My old memories were transferred to a different canvas, and the new ones will stay with me as well for many years.

SECTION SIX

The Canarías, Spain; Morocco, North Africa

Section 6, Canarias, Spain; Morocco
Cave of Hercules, archeological cave complex located in
Northern Morocco, where the Mediterranean Sea meets
the Atlantic Ocean. The cave opening overlooking the
sea resembles the contours of the African continent.
Photo credit: Janet Spiegel©2019.

I Found My Synagogue in a Lava Tube

As I recounted in an earlier story, "Getting the Balance Right," I had been inside a lava tube once before. Inside that tube, amazingly, was a thousand-year-old rain forest that cut right through the Kilauea volcano in the Hawaiian Islands. In recent years, that volcano erupted so forcefully that it destroyed everything in its wake. In fact, the eruption did so much damage that the Hawaii Volcanic National Park had to be closed for a long, long time.

* * * *

Decades have passed, and I am standing with my daughter, Janet, at the entrance to another natural wonder on a different island. This time it is a black lava tube on Lanzarote, in the Canarias (Canary Islands in English). These islands, infamous for dealings with pirates in past centuries, are part of Spain, but they are autonomous. It has taken six days at sea on the Atlantic Ocean to travel here from Barbados, our first stop.[39] I am with my daughter, Janet. Here, an immensely talented man has joined forces with nature to create an aesthetic, unexpectedly spiritual, environment carved from the black rocks inside.

His name is César Manrique, and, although I had never before heard of him, he is an internationally known and respected artist. His life's work—he has since passed away—is built on the premise that art and nature in combination cannot be surpassed. His projects are large scale, and their effect is deeply moving. His major work is intentionally on Lanzarote, and they have brought fame—and tourists, with an accompanying boost to the economy—to an island created from ground-up, rocky soil as well. The landscape is dotted with small settlements of white, adobe-style houses clustered together on the black land, with a little greenery flourishing here and there.

My daughter, who rock climbs as a sport, jokes that I have also become a rock climber in Manrique's lava tube. She calls it "scrambling." I would call it something else—OMG—stooping as low to the ground as possible and clutching on to the jagged rocks like a railing as I climb the many steps carved further and further into the black tube. Soon my fears of falling disappear as I am overwhelmed by the aesthetic experience created by a master artist.

Manrique and his team have enlarged a natural opening in the rock in the shape of a perfect oval, so that those who enter the lava tube discover a magnificent view of the ocean and the looming mountains beyond. This exquisite sight from outside is reflected in a large, sky blue pool amid the rocks, bestowing a unity with the outside world on the lava tube's environment. The water continually flows from the lava tube to the sea, so that the level of the water rises and falls with the tide. As I look at the pool with the eyes of a rabbi who serves as a *dayan* in a rabbinic court, I realize that, unintentionally, Manrique has created a natural *mikveh* (body of water for ritual purification).

And when I look at the water and surrounding rocks more closely, I see that there are living things in this pool—tiny, albino spider-crabs, as small as spiders, but they are actually crabs—that keep the water clean.

We climb more stairs, further into the tube. And then we enter a huge space carved out of the rocks, or maybe it is a natural space, a bubble in the lava tube. I gasp. My daughter gasps. The immense ceiling is so high. It is dimly lit. Benches carved from the black rock and accented with white plaster backs descend down a long, sloped aisle to what seems to be—a stage?—at its base. There are benches on the other side of the aisle too. Seating, we learn, for 1200 people. Classical concerts are given here at regular intervals. The acoustics are terrific, and the space has been wired for sound and additional lighting. Amazing.

It is an awesome space; it feels like a cathedral. I imagine that it is a synagogue at *Rosh Hashana*. On the stage, the *bima*, my mind projects an altar and there, just behind it, an Ark holding the Torah scrolls. The rabbi—is it me? A few of my colleagues taking turns with me, sharing the service?—and a cantor are there. A choir? Of course. Are there people sitting on the benches? Throughout my visit to the Canary Islands, I have looked for Jewish history, for any evidence that there is still a synagogue in these islands (there is a small one in Las Palmas, and the Torah scroll that was once in Tenerife was sent there; however, the synagogue's door is unmarked, and, in the brief time I was in Las Palmas, I could not find it).

Once, even before the Spanish and Portuguese Inquisitions, there was a humble Jewish community on this island, Lanzarote. Later there was a prosperous community of Portuguese Jews who fled their own land and built this island's economy. Once…

I take a deep breath. At this moment in time, just for this beautiful moment, I have found what could serve as a synagogue deep in the rocks. Complete with *mikveh*—and catering service. And my daughter is by my side. Outside the sun is shining.

Flowering Plants in a Lunar-like Landscape

*I*n the previous story, I wrote about the immense, cathedral-like environment carved out of a lava tube on Canary Island's Lanzarote by inspired nature-artist César Manrique. Among many other projects, he also created a huge, park-like, otherworldly environment, *Jardin de Cactus*. It featured more than 1,100 species of cacti planted in what was a disused quarry—until Manrique, who is also an architect, decided to marry nature with art and vice-versa. He and his talented team created a jaw-dropping garden of carefully landscaped and tended cacti, accented with red rocks, bridges, paved paths, and even pools at different levels.

These are not little or even medium-sized cacti, oh no! Everything is grand in scale, plants that have been nurtured in the volcanic soil for many years. They range, according to the *Jardin's* information, "from towering saguaros and spiny over-sized globes to more unusual species that resemble giant white maggots, thrusting asparagus spears, prickly mounds of broccoli, or dark green corals and sea anemones." All have been planted in close proximity to one another in artistic patterns. The result, which took twenty years to complete, is astoundingly beautiful.

It was springtime when we visited, my daughter and I. And so many of the cacti were in bloom. It took my breath away. The word "awesome" seemed almost inadequate.

For me, visiting the *Jardin de Cactus* was a Heschel moment. Rabbi Abraham Joshua Heschel has long captured my imagination with his concept of "radical amazement," which thankfully continues to influence every day of my life. As Heschel wrote about in his stellar books, *God in Search of Man: A Philosophy of Judaism*, and *Moral Grandeur and*

Spiritual Audacity, that we should live our lives with a sense of wonder: to be spiritual is to be amazed.[40] We should get up every morning with an appreciation of being alive, he explained, with a sense of awe at the mystery of life, and the desire to celebrate it.

That sense of wonder certainly resonated in me at the *Jardin*. It was springtime when my daughter and I visited. So many of the cacti were in bloom in response to the balmy weather, it took my breath away. Although I understood that cacti have many practical uses in the desert, I didn't know that cacti are actually flowering plants. The word "awesome" seemed almost inadequate.

I did know about the "monocarpic" century plant, so biologically labelled because it is a cactus said to bloom only once in 100 years (although some century plants have been known to bloom much sooner, perhaps in a few decades, depending on the climate, soil, and care they get). Unfortunately, after the century plant (horticulturally categorized as an "Agave Americana") blooms, it usually dies. I took a long look at one of the *Jardin's* century plants; it reminded me of male worker bees who, once they mate with the queen bee, also die after this moment of glory.

It also reminded me that I still have a way to go before my final bloom. My human generation seems to have an unusual number of centenarians, so it's comforting to know that at least a few century plants, like most cacti, are repeat bloomers.

Fortunately, most humans have the capacity to be repeat bloomers, as indeed César Manrique's many projects testify. The *Jardin de Cactus* was his last project—his final artistic bloom—completed in the 1990s. Two years later, he died in a car crash. His beautiful creations, however, live on in the volcanic soil. Truly awesome!

Awesome too, was the excitement of one of our fellow tourists, a retired surgeon from California, who was almost dancing with joy as he checked out the cacti in the garden. "I have two greenhouses at home, with 400 varieties of cacti growing," he exulted. "And I can identify so many of the cacti in the *Jardin*. Of course, my cacti are little. I love to take care of them."

"Do they bloom yet?" I asked this brilliant man, who had become our friend; after so many years of doctoring, he still loved to care for living things.

"Not yet," he replied. "But now I know they will."

Our tour guide almost had to pull him out of the garden to rejoin the bus. He simply didn't want to leave the cacti blooming, as if just for us, on a lovely spring day.

Who Can Forget The Taste of Jam?

A paperback copy of a French-language book etched in my
memory was entitled *Le Gout des Confitures* ("The Taste
of Jam").[41] It was authored by Bob Oré, a Moroccan-born, Jewish
businessman I knew long ago in his art-dealing capacity in Montreal.
Forced by the Arab hostility toward Jews aroused in 1948 when Israel
was declared a state—an anger that became dangerous when Morocco
ceased to be a French protectorate in 1956—he sought a new version
of his life in other countries. After first attempting to settle in both
France and Israel, he immigrated to French-speaking Montreal. Like
many immigrants, his book explains, he never felt completely at home
anywhere other than the land of his birth. In France, he was not French
enough; in Israel, he was not a *sabra*; in Quebec, he was not *Québécois*,
but at least, *au moins*, he was not *un anglais* (although he spoke both
English and French fluently).

His yearning for the sunny skies, the flowers, the multiple cultures
and languages of Morocco, and especially the friendships scattered
around the world, express the loss of what was once near and dear felt
by first-generation immigrants everywhere.

In the years before Oré found his way to Canada, with lots of
business acumen to sustain him, some 250,000 Jews lived in Morocco.
They had lived in that North African country for centuries, even
thousands of years, many emigrating there long before the Romans
conquered Israel and destroyed the Temple in the early common era.
Native to Morocco when those first Jewish immigrants arrived were
the Berbers, and the Jews got along with that indigenous population

very well. In fact, a considerable number of Berbers even converted to Judaism. Morocco grew prosperous.

In the fifteenth and sixteenth centuries CE, the Spanish Inquisition brought a different group of Jewish immigrants to the island, this time *Conversos* fleeing for their lives. Seemingly converted to Christianity, most of them lived secret lives as Jews. Even so, the long arm of the Inquisition tried to reach into Morocco to punish the secret Jews they detected, but with little success. The Moroccan population did not cooperate. Why disturb the country's prosperity, aided in large measure by the Jews?

In 1910, the archives of the long-ago Inquisition in Morocco were revealed in a lecture to the British Historical Society by an eminent scholar: His detailed research showed that, although there were numerous harsh interrogations, few were prosecuted, and "only" four were burned at the stake, one of them a woman. Nevertheless, the Jewish community continued to build and celebrate a substantial Jewish life.

Today, a large drawing by a contemporary artist is prominently displayed in the small, four-room Jewish museum in Casablanca. It depicts many of the Inquisition's "penitents." They are being forced to repent for the crime of remaining Jewish, and so they wear tall, pointed hats to mark their humiliation and reduced status. Some penitents are depicted with ropes around their necks. Since they have renounced Judaism, they will suffer an easier death: they will be strangled before being burnt at the stake.

The museum itself portrays a different message. Attractively built in recent years, the museum is sponsored by King Hassan II. Like his father, King Mohammed VI, before him, who tried to protect Moroccan Jews from the French Vichy regime during World War II, Hassan promotes harmony and toleration in his kingdom. At the entrance, a large plaque bearing the king's signature and commemorating the opening of the museum, proclaims that all peoples and religions may live in harmony and peace together in Morocco. There is a picture of the head of the Jewish community shaking hands with a government official.

Billed as the only Jewish museum in the Arab world (except perhaps for the ancient *Genizah*—depository for fragmented sacred books—in Cairo, Egypt), it has multiple cases filled with magnificent antique Berber jewelry. Photographs of Jews living happily in Morocco decorate the walls throughout the four rooms. A large *bima* (platform) from a Casablanca synagogue that formerly existed stands in the middle of the largest room. I climbed the steps to the *bima* and looked over the dark-wood railing, a rabbi addressing the congregation that wasn't there. The ark holds three large Torahs clothed in soft, velvet mantles, which rather surprised me. I had expected cylindrical Sephardic Torahs. Some of the most interesting contents of the museum can be viewed on multiple sites on the Internet. Many of the artifacts depicting Jewish life, however, are from the 1950s.

But where are the Jews now? The Moroccan climate is great; the food is fantastic; the people are welcoming; the newly restored but small synagogue is there. It provides a considerable contrast to Casablanca's magnificent Hassan II Mosque, the largest in Africa and fifth largest in the world. Completed in 1993, it was elaborately built at such great cost (reputed to be $800 million), with hand-carvings decorating every inch and a retractable roof (there is no air-conditioning), its construction nearly bankrupted Morocco, and the citizenry was taxed to pay for it. It has a capacity of 25,000 inside and another 80,000 outside for large holidays like Ramadan. As I was guided through, I was awed by its immensity—the minaret is sixty stories high and faces the Atlantic Ocean—and could only imagine what it must look like when devout Muslims fill it for prayer.

But the synagogue is empty. When necessary—a funeral, a *yarzheit* (memorial prayer), another ritual event—the remaining Jews of Casablanca gather a *minyan* (the requisite ten people to hold a service). The diminishing Jewish community celebrates the High Holy Days as best they can. This year for Passover, there was a colorful poster showing that a *Seder* (a ritual feast celebrating the biblical liberation from slavery in Egypt) would take place at a stunning hotel in picturesque Marrakesh. The food would be kosher, and the eight-day stay would only cost $1590 Euros ($1900 US) per person (considered very reasonable).

Still, most of the Jews who come to Morocco are tourists, and Morocco is actively trying to promote its Jewish tourist trade. The

101

children of Moroccan parents and grandparents come to visit the graves, but they don't live there, in what is essentially an Arab culture. Dress is not legislated, although most Arab women I saw wore traditional dress, including the *hijab* (head scarf). Their tunics were colorful, and few black *abayas* (cloaks) or face veils were seen.

The bottom line? An estimated 2,500 Jews now live in Morocco, the majority in Casablanca. Most of them are elderly and some infirm. Unless the community is reinforced, it will soon disappear by attrition. What will remain is the memory—the taste, the *gout*, for what was left behind, the love for what has been, but is not now, and can never be again: the *je ne sais quoi* of long-lost memories.

Finding Life After The Digitized Dead

*J*ust as my daughter and I had visited the lovingly restored, small synagogue in Casablanca, it was important to us to visit the old synagogue in Tangier, located by winding our way through the maze of alleys adjacent to the bazaar (the *shouk* or marketplace). By pre-arrangement, our guide pressed a buzzer, and a custodian opened the gate.

As in the Casablanca synagogue, services are held only on the High Holy Days, but a *minyan* is usually gathered together for other ritual necessities. Similarly, too, the Tangier synagogue was immaculate but, other than the custodian, empty of people. Only this lone synagogue remains now, yet once there were seventeen synagogues in Tangier. The custodian showed us a hand-made map charting the locations where they once stood.

The adjoining graveyard was sadly in ruined condition, but the names carved into the headstones, as well as the actual locations of the graves, had been gathered and thoughtfully digitized. We spent some time with the custodian poring over the print-out. Would we recognize any of these names as possible ancestors of Moroccan Jews we had met in Montreal?

"Do you have a donation for the synagogue?" the custodian asked.

* * * *

After this moving experience, and with my wallet a little lighter, we took a much-needed break for lunch. The décor in the cozy restaurant was, well, elaborately Moroccan, and the food fantastic. We especially enjoyed the *pastillas*, which each chef seems to make deliciously different.

All the *pastillas* seem to contain chicken, are artistically breaded, and fried (or baked). This may sound like down-home, Southern fried chicken in the US, but it's not in the same universe.

We had reserved the afternoon for souvenir shopping in the bazaar, with its winding streets and alleyways. This is an area where you absolutely need a guide—unless you enjoy having four or five would-be sellers constantly dangling merchandise in front of your face. If you have a guide, they back off. Then you feel bad because you know they need to make a living.

Along with the abundant trivia, there were many quality shops in the bazaar. Our guide knew all of the owners standing at the shop doors—there was much calling out of familiar names and expansive back-slapping—and he led us to a shop specializing in beautifully made antique silver, quite obviously rare and expensive. I fell in love with a single candlestick that had been crafted to look as if its base and stem were swirling flames, each flame inset with coral. The initial price started at $5,000, and slowly went down to $2,000 by the time I was going out the door. I am not a haggler; there was only one candlestick, and I wanted a pair. In any case, it was beyond my budget. Way beyond!

As I edged out the door, I noticed that lying on the chair holding it open were a few velvet *tefillin* (phylacteries) and *tallit* (prayer shawl) bags and—a little *kippah* (skullcap). It was tan suede with many little glass insets outlined in navy blue. Some of them were missing, but there was a red pom-pom on top. True, it was matted together, but I could wash it and brush it.

"Where is this from?" I asked.

"Oh, it's used," the sales attendant said scornfully. "It's from the synagogue…when they renovated. They want to sell these things. But they're used. We sell antiques."

"All antiques are used," I replied. "Only they've been used longer than this *kippah*." The attendant didn't know that I have been collecting *kippahs* (new ones!) from synagogues in the many countries I have visited.

"It's damaged, you know," he told me. Some of the glass insets are missing."

"But this *kippah* is authentic," I said softly. "It's small. Maybe a

Bar Mitzvah boy wore it, right here in Morocco. Long ago. So...How much?"

"What you want to give," he said, smiling broadly. "You know, it's a donation for the synagogue."

So I took another 20 Euros out of my wallet. And I was happy.

When I got home, I let the *kippah* soak overnight in a mixture of baking soda and warm water. In the morning I brushed the suede until it looked like new, and I untangled and trimmed the red pom-pom until it looked perky and festive.

And one day—maybe at *Rosh Hashana* (the Jewish New Year)—I will celebrate by wearing a Moroccan *Bar Mitzvah* boy's *kippah*, crafted with artistry, and restored with love, to a synagogue service in sunny California. In my *kavannah* (mindful intention) before prayer, I will be giving continuity to the spiritual life of a Moroccan boy hopefully too young to be among the digitally recorded dead.

Tangier: Location, Location, Location!

*E*ven though Humphrey Bogart and Lauren Bacall didn't star in a movie about Tangier (who has not seen their fictional romance in Casablanca unfold on a cinema screen?), this busy port-city in Northwestern Morocco has a history to rival Casablanca. Its location at the western entrance to the Strait of Gibraltar—right where the Mediterranean Sea meets the Atlantic Ocean—has given Tangier a trade advantage over the years to the extent that in 1928 it was deemed an international city. Its history as an important port goes back to the time of the Phoenicians in the 10th century BCE. History, history, history!

And even though Tangier today is a lively, modern city with attractive landscaping, affluent neighborhoods, and important projects, my daughter and I wanted to visit the old *medina* with its colorful mélange of shops and signs. Although it was, in part, once a thriving Jewish neighborhood in Tangier, none of the shops retained names that were likely to be Jewish anymore.

Unlike other cities in Morocco, Tangier never had a *mellah* (a walled and gated area where Jews were required to live, ostensibly for their own protection) similar to the European ghettos. Nevertheless, the Jewish inhabitants of Morocco understood that they were living in an Arab, mainly Islamic neighborhood, and that certain restrictions applied to non-Islamic residents who lived in Arab lands, including Morocco. Although Jews and Christians were both respected as "People of the Book," they understood that they were considered inferior to Muslims and expected to defer to them in many ways. In addition, they had to pay a special tax for the privilege of living in Morocco. Basically, they were second-class citizens referred to as *dhimmis* (meaning "protected" status in exchange for paying a levied tax).

Most of the time, the different religious groups understood their place in Moroccan society and got along very well, but, regrettably, over the centuries (the eighth century and again in the fifteenth century in the city of Fez, in particular), some large massacres of Jews took place. Centuries later, during the World War II Nazi regime in Germany and the pro-Nazi, Vichy government in France (Morocco, remember, was a French protectorate), many civil restrictions on Jews were put into place—despite the best efforts of the Moroccan King to prevent them.

When World War II ended in 1945, and after its own War of Independence, the State of Israel became a reality in 1948, Moroccan Jews found themselves targeted by a forceful Arab push for them to leave Morocco. Those who had the means immigrated to countries like Canada, France, and South America. At the same time, there was a strong biblical pull for the larger number of Moroccan Jews who for centuries had dreamed of making *Aliyah* (the ascent of return) to their spiritual home, Israel. And so the mid-twentieth century exodus to Israel began. Today, an estimated one million Jews of at least partial Moroccan ancestry are Israeli citizens—who still have tender feelings for Morocco.

SECTION SEVEN

Southeast Asia

Section 7, South East Asia
Incense coils in one of the oldest Buddhist Temples in Ho Chi Minh
city (Saigon) are often purchased by visitors. The coils are then hung
from the ceiling and believed to conduct accompanying prayers to
the divine. Individual names may be attached to the prayer coils.
Photo credit: Janet Spiegel©2018

Breaking an Ankle in Southeast Asia

*F*ortunately, Janet and I were able to get in a day's worth of touring before I broke my ankle by falling down a wide staircase in Singapore. At least, it was a beautiful flight of stairs, one of those architectural, fan-like creations without a railing, whose stairs appear to disappear one into the other. The staircase provided a lovely view of Singapore's gorgeous harbor, and distracted by the many ships from all over the world, I lost my footing near the bottom of the staircase. Somehow I managed to turn my head to avoid hitting it against the concrete half-wall that separated the stairs from the harbor. Apart from an ankle that appeared to be broken and a few scratches and scrapes, I was relatively unharmed. Definitely not dead.

Now the dilemma: Singapore is reputed to have excellent hospitals, but it was near the end of the afternoon. If I chose to seek medical care in Singapore, I would miss the last boarding call for our ship, and we had not yet registered on board. No, no, I didn't want the crew to sail without us for our cruise through Southeast Asia. We had come all the way from Los Angeles. And the next night was Passover—the first *Seder* (ritual feast; the word literally means "order" of the service)—and I was the rabbi.

"They have a medical clinic on the ship," I thanked all the concerned people who wanted to convey me to the nearest hospital, and somehow, supported by my daughter and an ACE bandage hiding in her purse, managed to hobble my way to the ship, which, thank God, was reasonably close by.

As a result, I got to see Southeast Asia mainly from a) the ship's deck as we entered or left a port; b) from the backseat of a touring car or taxi large enough to accommodate a folding wheelchair (kindly lent to me by the ship's staff); c) from the more adventurous experiences of the other passengers; and d) the informational lectures and films shown regularly on board.[42] The Jewish passengers didn't mind at all that their rabbi conducted Passover and other services or discussion groups with a big, grey boot on her right foot.

Prior to falling down the stairs, I did get an initial look at Singapore. First of all, it is a modern, prosperous city-island—a republic with a constitution, an elected president, and executive, legislative, and judiciary branches. Everywhere you look, the city is sparkling clean, but the laws have harsh consequences if you break them, even little ones: Do not chew gum in Singapore! There are dire penalties, including death, for more severe crimes.

Society is very regulated, including the locations where people can live at different ages and stages, according to our guide, but the citizens I spoke to in the brief time I was there seemed happy and secure. Generally, people said, it is very pleasant to live in Singapore. Beauty, too, is an integral part of the culture, as the magnificent, costly condos surrounding the harbor can attest. Although these condos are mainly foreign-owned, foreigners cannot own the land on which they are built, which is leased. Singaporeans have a lot of *sechel* (knowledge, common sense)!

Our tour guide explained that Singapore's children are taught in school that they have to be competitive, to be ahead of the curve. Why? Singapore is not blessed with natural resources (such as oil, minerals etc.) like some other countries of the world, and so Singapore's young people have to make up for it with education and creative innovation. The educational system itself is excellent. Of course, location and geography are resources too. Singapore's harbor is packed with ships, visiting tourists, and plenty of commerce.

Since I had no opportunity to look into what Jewish life there might be in Singapore, I resorted to investigating it from a variety of sources on the Internet and discovered that Jewish life is, indeed, quite healthy.[43] The first Jewish immigrants—Arabic-speaking Baghdadi traders from Calcutta who soon adopted the Malay language—arrived during the

18th and 19th centuries, while Singapore was still under Ottoman rule. A few of their descendants still exist.

In 1841, they were allowed to build a small Sephardic synagogue, *Maghain Aboth*. Naturally, the Ashkenazi Jews who arrived as the century progressed wanted their own synagogue, and eventually they got one (*Chesed-El*) in 1905. By the time the Japanese occupied Singapore in 1942, it had a Jewish population of about 1500, most of whom were sent to POW camps. After World War II, those who survived migrated to various Western countries.

Happily, favorable economic developments in the late 1980s attracted many Ashkenazi Jews. As the Jewish community grew to 2,500 soon after the turn of the century, another synagogue was needed, this time a vibrant Reform synagogue without walls (United Hebrew Congregation). In addition, a forty-million dollar campus, the Sir Manasseh Meyer International School, was in progress in Sembawang (a residential town in the North of Singapore), to provide education for Jewish children.

Singapore is a place I would love to visit again. On both my feet.

Thailand: A Welcoming Place for Jews

*I*f you are of my generation or that of my children, most likely you have watched the film, "Anna and the King of Siam," many times over the years, or even had the good fortune to see the theatrical version. Remember Yul Brynner? So naturally I was looking forward to visiting Thailand (formerly Siam). It is still a kingdom.

Another reason for wanting to go ashore is that Thailand is not only religiously tolerant, but it has been a welcoming place for Jews since 1601. That's when the first Jewish merchants (such as Abraham Navarro, English East India company) got there. Their presence was noted by Spanish missionaries. In 1890, some European families settled in Bangkok. In the 1920s, it was a place of refuge for Russian Jews from Harbin, and in the 1930s for German Jews escaping from the Nazis. Then, during World War I, Jews fled from Syria and Lebanon. In the 1950s and 60s, sufficient Jews arrived from America, Iraq, Afghanistan, and Iran so that by 1964, the Jewish community was well established. In the 1970s, many Israeli soldiers or those seeking business opportunities enlarged the community. Today, despite terror threats, thousands of Jews travel to Thailand every year.

A third reason is that Thailand has friendly relations with Israel, with formal diplomatic relations beginning in 1954. Over the years, a great deal of cooperation in agricultural, educational, and cultural matters has taken place. Bangkok boasts an Israeli Embassy, and there is a Royal Thai Embassy in Tel Aviv. Many young Israelis enjoy visiting Thailand to relax after their military service. Chabad is an orthodox presence in various cities. While the actual Thai Jewish community is a little less than a thousand people, that number swells during the High Holy Days and Passover.

Although I would have loved to disembark and explore Thailand at least a little, I was under strict medical orders not to move my ankle off the ship for a week so that the bones would stay in place. So there I remained, together with my grey boot, the folding wheelchair, and the library books aboard the ship.[44]

When the passengers returned from their nine-hour trip to Bangkok (where most of the Jewish community resides), they said it was a wonderful experience.

Cambodia and Chabad

*W*ith my generation's memories of the Killing Fields of the communist Khmer Rouge,[45] I was not keen on visiting our next port of call in Cambodia, which is also a kingdom. During this horrific genocide which began in 1975, the revolutionary *Khmer Rouge*, led by Pol Pot, forcibly moved city dwellers to the countryside to become agricultural workers. Hundreds of thousands of the educated middle class were tortured and executed. Others starved to death or died from disease. The total death toll was estimated to be between almost two to three million. After the Vietnamese took Phnom Penh in 1979, a guerilla war ensued. Not until 1994 did the *Khmer Rouge* guerillas surrender. Pol Pot died in his jungle hideout in 1998. Most senior members of *Khmer Rouge* were finally charged with crimes against humanity in 2007.[46]

No substantial Jewish community was ever established in Cambodia. The country was and is mostly populated by Theraveda Buddhists, but also some Muslim Chan, as well as ethnic Chinese and Vietnamese. So I was not too disappointed that I still had to stay aboard when we sailed into Sihanoukville, a rather unkempt Cambodian town. However, it did have an airport, the reason we had stopped there since some of our shipmates were making a side-trip by air to see an ancient Cambodian Temple, *Angkor Wat* (Capital of Temples), reputed to have one of the largest Buddhas in the world. After their trip, they would rejoin our ship. As it happens, it was very hot, and there were long tourist lines at the Temple site, so everyone said that it was a good thing that I couldn't go.

Very few Jews—perhaps 200—reside in Cambodia currently, but

those who do mostly live in the populous and more affluent capital, Phnom Penh, once known as the pearl of Asia. Here Chabad welcomes both residents and tourists with open arms. My hat is off to Chabad, whose orthodox rabbis courageously establish themselves in remote and difficult places, and on Friday night in Cambodia serve an average of twenty-five dinners to any Jew who comes. Chabad is an acronym for *Chochma* (Wisdom), *Bina* (Understanding), and *Da'at* (Knowledge), attributes of the Divine at the top of the mystical Tree of Life.

Vietnam: The Future is Now!

*M*y most memorable moment in Vietnam was being pushed—the moment my guide spied a small opening—in my wheelchair across a very, very busy street to a grassy boulevard where a huge statue of Ho Chi Minh towered over the park. In the latter part of the 19th century, what later became an independent Vietnam was colonized as French Indo China, a French protectorate, and French was then the fashionable language to speak in Saigon, its foremost city.

Most Jewish settlers arrived soon after the French colonization of Vietnam. By 1902, the *École française d'Extrême-Orient* (French School of the Far East) was active in Hanoi, the *Alliance Israelite Universelle* was thriving in Haiphong in the 1920s, and the US Consul in Vietnam, Henry Samuel Waterman, whose warnings about the threatening growth of communism went unheeded by the US government, was Jewish.[47]

By 1939, the combined Jewish communities in French Indo China numbered about 1,000 people, some of them in the military or foreign legion. Sadly in 1940, the antisemitic Vichy French implemented their "Statutes on Jews" on French Indo China (imposing limitations on Jews in a wide range of professions, educational institutions, business, and banking interests). Fortunately, at the end of World War II, these statutes were repealed.

At the same time, Ho Chi Minh, who was born in France, became the leader of the Viet Minh independence movement in 1941. Although he established the Communist Democratic Republic of Vietnam in 1945, he did not finally defeat the French Union until 1954 at the battle of Dien Bien Phu. Notably, French Premier Pierre Mendes France, who was Jewish, helped negotiate the pull-out. Although Vietnam had now achieved independence, the country was separated into a communist north and a capitalist south. It was a divided Vietnam.

Saigon, South Vietnam's foremost city, was renamed after Ho Chi Minh. So now it is Ho Chi Minh City. While officially Vietnam is an atheist state, the majority of the South Vietnamese practice either Buddhism, Taoism, or Confucianism. They may also practice *tam giao*, a folk religion combining all three. Most of the Christians are Catholic. Most of the Jews in Vietnam departed with the French.

Soon there was another war, a disastrous war for all its participants, between the US and communist Vietnam. The Vietnam War lasted for twenty long years from 1955 to 1975. Although the US and North Vietnam ended hostilities in 1973, North and South Vietnam did not conclude an agreement until 1975.

It should be mentioned that during the Vietnam War, some 30,000 Jewish Americans served the US, and from 1977 to 1979, Israel's Prime Minister, Menachem Begin, allowed 360 Vietnamese "boat people," refugees fleeing the communists to enter Israel, granting them full Israeli citizen rights. Although only a few Jews live year round in Vietnam today, thousands of Jewish tourists visit for business purposes, or for the High Holy Days, or during Passover, and, it almost goes without saying that Chabad is there to welcome them with religious services and kosher meals in Ho Chi Minh City.[48]

Now, almost thirty-five years after the Vietnam War, my daughter, Janet, and I dutifully smiled as our guide snapped the required, it seemed—he was so insistent—photos of us with the statue, and we admired the park's beautiful flowers. My heart finally stopped pounding from the wheelchair ride across the street because whether one will actually get to the other side or not is anyone's guess. The traffic in Vietnam is unbelievable with a veritable brigade of non-stop motorcycles whizzing through the roads. Speeding along with them are an unceasing stream of cars and even pedicabs and occasional carts drawn by horses. By seemingly tacit agreement everyone plunges into the traffic, and once you have entered it, you don't stop. No! You keep going and simply curve around each other at the right moment, even if you are driving in different directions. At least that is my impression.

119

The roar of the traffic is echoed by the non-stop energy we experienced everywhere in Saigon, so palpable you could almost hold it in your hand. The Vietnamese are going somewhere fast! Making up for lost time! The city itself is modern and stunning, the shopping areas in the city's center almost like a Rodeo Drive in Los Angeles. There is interesting architecture, as well as art galleries and educational institutions. South Vietnam has built itself up amazingly in the intervening years.

There are memorial museums, too, with narratives that are sad and largely unflattering to the United States of America when they recount the Vietnam War. Generally speaking, however, the Vietnamese today are far more interested in building their future than wallowing in the past.

Darwin: Gateway to Southeast Asia

*M*y experience of Darwin (originally called Palmerston) revealed a very different climate—tropical in nature—and landscape to other areas of Australia I had visited on a prior trip. It also revealed a long-held secret. Darwin, which served as an important Allied military supply and re-fueling base, was severely bombed by the Japanese in 1942, only a couple of months after the devastating December, 1941 attack on the Pearl Harbor fleet that brought the US into World War II. The result of the Darwin attack was destruction of the planes on the ground, supplies, people. Everything. Apparently, this Japanese bombing was subsequently kept secret by the Allies to prevent terrorizing a population already upset by what had happened at Pearl Harbor. Eventually, the town was rebuilt. That is when it was re-named Darwin, after the naturalist, Charles Darwin, of course.

Since it is a small city, we didn't expect much traffic the beautiful sunny day our cruise ship stopped at the port, but, to our surprise, the UK's Prince Charles and entourage were taking a look too.

Billed as "The Gateway to Southeast Asia" on the Timor Sea and known for its "culture, crocodiles, and cuisine," Darwin is the capital and chief port of Australia's Northern Territory.[49] It is situated on a low peninsula northeast of the entrance to its harbor. Although this city at the "top end" of the continent seems well settled in 2019, its modern houses well maintained, and its attractive shopping areas accommodating, Darwin has been devastated over the years not only by bombing attacks but by repeated cyclones. In 1974, Cyclone Tracy leveled nearly all of the city a second time. Again it was rebuilt.

So you can understand why no Jewish life has ever been established in Darwin. Australian Jewish communities have been reluctant to settle there because of Darwin's history of building and rebuilding in the wake of disaster. There has been enough of that in Jewish history. However, since the area is surrounded by beautiful parkland and trails, it has always attracted a large aboriginal population. Pastoral lands are also being developed for mining and oil exploration, and Darwin continues to service the armed forces.

In fact, there were two museums dedicated to each of the World Wars. But Janet and I chose instead to visit an absolute jewel of a museum featuring aboriginal art.[50] It turned out to be far beyond our expectations, one of the most creative and attractive exhibits we had seen throughout our cruise through Southeast Asia. What I hadn't expected to find was the clever intermix of modern technology with aboriginal history in Australia. Aboriginal rights are a big issue in Australia, as they are in many other lands.

There was also a secondary exhibit that documented the effects of Cyclone Tracy on Darwin—but also the courageous rebuilding of the town. No more houses that left their front facades open to better enjoy the elements and the view were built any more.

After the exhibit, we savored the exceptional cuisine of Darwin at—guess what?—an Italian restaurant. It was for sale because, now that the Canadian owner and his wife had two kids, they wanted to return to Toronto to be near their families. People are more the same than they are different everywhere.

Linking to the Ancestors (Bali)

*T*he balmy weather and the vivid greenness of surrounding nature in Los Angeles in the spring, especially after a week or two of rain, remind me of the paradisal gentleness of nature in Bali (if you put aside the heaps of plastic that have accumulated on their once pristine beaches).

Surrounded by Muslim neighbors on other Indonesian islands, according to Professor Google, there are more than 17,000 islands in all, with a population of almost 264 million people. Muslims account for 225 million, or 87 percent, of this population. The government of Indonesia does not include Judaism among the six officially recognized religions; the very small number of Jews (about 200) practice in secrecy.[51] Bali is a predominantly Hindu island and welcomes people of all religions.

Balinese Hinduism (an amalgamation of Hinduism, Buddhism, and native animism) places great stress on connection to ancestors. For the Balinese, this beautiful island will always be the land of their ancestors. "Our young people always come back," an aging Balinese man told me. "They go away to get educated—doctors, lawyers, teachers—but they always come back to Bali. Because this is where their ancestors are."

The roads to the main cities and marketplaces may be overcrowded with tourists now, but in at least one remote village, tradition is honored. Once a year the villagers unearth the buried bones of their ancestors and wash them. Then, satisfied they have honored their predecessors' memory, they rebury the clean bones. In the ancient Balinese way, they pay respect to those who have come before them.

In rural houses of worship, the large statues that represent the many gods of their religious mythology, are draped by the local people with cloaks and hats made of gold cloth or other fine materials. Food and drink are set before them as if they were still present in this world. Of course, the local people "know" that statues are not really gods; they are symbols, representations of their belief system, and they are paying homage to these beliefs.

I bought two shadow puppets made in the traditional way from leather (not plastic, though these were available as well) and hand-painted to represent these mythological gods. They have exotic names and stories that the Balinese people well know and treasure. For the moment, they sit in a tall vase in my home, souvenirs of a country blessed by nature but already caught in the throes of environmental change. Yet the casual tourist, like myself in a brief visit over two days, is likely to feel that Bali will be all right. Because the children will always come back.

While in Bali, I kept thinking of the opening verses—"Patriarchs"—of the central prayer of the Jewish religion: the *Amidah* (the standing prayer). We Jews, too, know where the ancestors are: Abraham, Isaac, and Jacob, Sarah, Rebekah, Rachel and Leah. Abraham bought the Cave of Machpelah to bury Sarah, a purchase in silver coins recorded in the Torah. Joseph carried his father's bones back to the Holy Land. And the children will always come back to honor and protect their memory.[52]

The Philippines: A Memorable Connection

Two things stand out about my visit to Manila, the capital city and economic and cultural hub of the Philippines located on the island of Luzon: the Spanish restoration of the old town in Manila, and the Chinese "Village of the Ancestors" located a little way past the American government buildings. The Chinese Village literally "houses" elaborate vaults for Chinese elders who have passed away. In each of the substantial, beautifully decorated houses, vaults contain the long-deceased bodies of their ancestors, and lots of room for those who come to mourn their relatives and perhaps stay a while. There are several winding streets of these house-vaults, all beautifully landscaped and maintained. It's almost as if there is a competition for who can have the most stunning house and vault. Security guards are also visible because the houses of the dead contain many valuables.

It was an eerie but deeply touching experience—it brought tears to our eyes—to explore this area to the extent we could. The reverence for one's ancestors reminded me of the ancient town in Bali where the people excavate and wash the bones of their ancestors yearly before replacing them in their graves. Or the lengthy genealogies we really shouldn't skip in the Hebrew Bible.

The Restoration of the Spanish Old Town reminded us of a gracious earlier time in the Philippines. Jews and Filipinos, after all, have a long history together. Spanish Jews, *Marranos*, first settled in Manila, the capital of the Philippines during the Spanish Inquisition. A couple of centuries later, in the late 1800s, French merchants, among them three Levy brothers from Alsace, arrived in Manila. It certainly seemed to be a popular place of refuge because the Spanish-American War brought

American Jews to the islands in the 1870s. In the next wave of those seeking relief from persecution came Jewish families from the Middle East and Turkey. Once again, after World War I, new groups of Jewish refugees from discrimination arrived from Russia.[53]

Both informative and touching in regard to the longstanding relationship between the Philippines and the Jews is a feature-length movie about international friendships born out of adversity and a love for freedom. The film's title is *An Open Door: Jewish Rescue in the Philippines*.[54] You can find the extended trailer on several sites on the Internet. It's an uplifting documentary (by film maker Noel M. Izon) about how a small Asian nation—the Philippines—was able to save 1,300 Jews as they fled the pogroms of Nazi Germany. The film juxtaposes the confluence of momentous historical events, such as the passage of the Nuremberg Laws on September 15, 1935, and exactly two months later, the inauguration of the Philippines as a Commonwealth of the United States. One door closes, and another opens, the movie teaches us.

Here are a few more facts:[55] In 1947, the Philippines was the only Asian nation to support the partition resolution of the United Nations creating a Jewish State in Palestine. Ten years later, in 1957, Israel and the Philippines established full diplomatic relations, and since 1969, Filipinos have not required visas to come to Israel, where a monument to the Philippine government stands as a "thank you" in Tel Aviv. A Jewish Association of the Philippines has been established, and a new synagogue (Syrian-Sephardic) has been built in Manila. I was aware that the Israeli government has sent humanitarian assistance to the Philippines in the wake of natural disasters. However, I didn't know that a contract exists between the Philippine Department of Defense and Israeli Aerospace to establish resources and technology for better safety in the South China Sea.

And I learned something else during my short visit to the Philippines: On US television screens and newspapers, the current president, Rodrigo Duterte, gets very bad press. He is portrayed as a dictator prone to violence, a tough guy who goes too far.

Yet, when I saw a filmed news segment that showed Duterte speaking to members of the Jewish Philippine community, it seemed to be a different story. Duterte is charismatic. "If you come into my country with drugs," he promised the audience, "I will kill you. Otherwise our country will become a failed state."[56] The audience applauded him heartily. And when my daughter, Janet, and I spoke to real-life Manila dwellers we met, they were all quick to defend their president. "Oh no," they told us, "a strong hand was needed to clean up Manila. He's done wonders for our country. We don't have to worry all the time about crime here. We can walk out of our homes at night and breathe freely. We can enjoy ourselves with our families. Duterte is good for us!"

I doubt that dictators are ever "good" for a population for any length of time, but in the moment, Manila dwellers are relieved to get into a jitney without getting mugged.

Leaving Hong Kong Misty-Eyed

*T*oday Janet and I are coming to the conclusion of a lengthy cruise from Los Angeles to Barbados to the countries of Southeast Asia, places I never dreamed I would visit. At this very moment, we are in the process of disembarking from this lovely "small" ship, which holds 450 passengers. And there he is, just as we dock at the port, a big smile wreathing his face, our Los Angeles friend and neighbor, Adam.

We all live in California, and proximity has lent a helping hand in developing our friendship, but Janet and I never expected how much we would appreciate our proximity to Adam in an unexpected part of the world: Hong Kong, now part of China. Not exactly next door to Los Angeles, but that's where we were hugging each other with real affection as we got off the ship.

It was actually Adam's wife, who (following our trip avidly on Facebook) clued us in by text message that Adam would be visiting Hong Kong on business the exact same day Janet and I would be briefly touring that Southeast Asian City as a prelude to flying home.

Since I still had a mending ankle—encased in a big boot—from falling down the stairs in Singapore, Janet had hired a private touring car for our meeting in Hong Kong. It was raining hard that day, and, as we drove through the city, the skies were so misty we couldn't see the much vaunted coastline at Repulse Bay Beach (we're told it's gorgeous), nor the tourist attractions of Victoria Peak. No way to tour Kowloon— we would not be able to view anything. Nor did we have a chance to explore the synagogues and communal sites of the Hong Kong Jewish community, which numbers about 5,000 people, mostly expatriates with business interests there.[57] We did see the rows and rows of impressively tall, rather skinny, buildings that line the port, almost like a cement jungle. On the positive side, we did have umbrellas when we left the car's protection, and we had each other. *Dayenu*, as we Jews say at Passover. It is enough.

My philosophy of traveling—and, indeed, of life—is that you make the most of what you have at that moment. So it didn't matter that much that we couldn't see the iconic skyline as we would have on a clear day, or that we couldn't go to the much vaunted beach. We were able to see what Hong Kong looked like on a rainy day.

So when we drank the "Western" coffee our tour guide had recommended in a tiny, "local color" restaurant with bright posters plastered to the walls, we thought it a great idea. Western coffee in Hong Kong is apparently intended to bring East and West together. How? By combining half tea (Eastern) and half coffee (Western) in one cup. Add milk and sugar and hope for worldwide peace and the restoration of your taste buds.

Janet, Adam, and I would have liked anything. Even the huge, plain, round buns (no butter or jam) that went with the beverage. It wasn't raining inside the café, and there we were, happy to have found each other on a lucky day in Hong Kong.

Adam insisted on accompanying us in Hong Kong until it was time to catch our flight at the city's very busy airport. So busy that it's nearly impossible to get on or off an elevator. An impassive crowd stands like a blockade in front of the elevator you absolutely need for where you have to go. No one moves to let anyone on or off. No one wants to lose his/her own space. Understandable when there are so many people for so comparatively few elevators. A young girl, talking loudly on her cell phone all the while knocked me into me in my wheelchair as she brushed past to get on the elevator (where she continued her conversation at the top of her lungs). So it seems like the current etiquette is to push your way through as fast as you can. It's an introduction to life in Hong Kong.

Hong Kong was once a British colony, and, while it is now officially part of China, the Hong Kong population still lives under a British system of law. Although the massive protests had not yet begun against a new Chinese law demanding extradition to China for detained people who would then be tried under Chinese law, the resistant strength of the Hong Kong population, along with its sheer numbers, could already be felt. The law has since been rescinded.

However, this city has another face, a sophisticated one; it can be really elegant, very elegant. The two finest restaurants at the airport had signs pointing in different directions that said, "Western food" or "Chinese food." We chose Chinese food, since, after all, we were in China. The meal and service were excellent, indeed, and we were in a great mood as we boarded our plane.

And then, serendipity! We were flying "business class," with well-padded chairs that stretched out into BEDS! So what if we didn't see much of Hong Kong! We could sleep in comfort in semi-privacy on that very, very long trip home. The flight attendants even gave us pajamas and slippers. We had hot meals! Wine! We were near the bathroom! Oh, thank you, doctor, for prescribing that I must fly home business class so that I could keep my foot up. Thank you, insurance company. Thank you, kind flight attendants.

Maybe I'll have the opportunity to visit Southeast Asia again one day and actually get to see Hong Kong when it isn't raining, but one thing is sure: It was almost worth a broken ankle just to experience that flight home.

SECTION EIGHT

Homecoming

Section 8, Homecoming
Family Judaica, Los Angeles, California
Photo credit: Ruth Barratt©2020.

Time to Put Hyphens on the Back Burner? Counting our Blessings.

Although I was born in Canada and proud to be a Canadian, I grew up with a soft spot in my heart for Americans because my family—and many other Canadians we knew—spent our vacation times mainly in the US. Living in Montreal as we did, the US border was only an hour away, and, after World War II (when travel to the US once again flowed freely), my mother, sister, and I spent several joyous summers on the banks of Lake Champlain in Plattsburgh, NY (unlike in Quebec, kids under sixteen could go to the movies there), with my Dad joining us on the weekends. Later, my college friends and I got to know New England well in bucolic places like Lake Placid and Lake George.

When I married, my husband and I spent our honeymoon in New York City, attending a different Broadway play every night for a week. We had a ski chalet in Mount Sutton, close to the Vermont border and often drove across for an afternoon. My in-laws were part of the "snowbird" crowd—my mother-in-law actually got a prescription from her doctor advising her husband she needed to spend the winter in Florida (still a popular destination for sun-seeking Montrealers). We were also grateful for our blessings, and we tried to give back to society in many ways.

As our four children grew, my husband and I became devotees of Maine's Ogunquit and Kennebunkport in the summer and then, venturing a little farther afield to Massachusetts, of Cape Cod. How we enjoyed the sandy beach and tranquil waters of West Dennis and sometimes the daunting, cold waves of Nauset Beach! For several years, we explored the Cape's artistic locations and innovators, its renowned aquatic museum in Wood's Hole, and its marine cuisine. We loved American holidays like July 4th, when the population would always stand as one and place their hands on their hearts while lustily singing the National Anthem.

"Americans are patriotic," we would say approvingly. "Americans make a lot of noise. Americans are a lot of fun." Canadians, by contrast, were more circumspect, we thought, more modest in their expressions of fealty to their country. Not everyone knew all the words to our own National Anthem, "O Canada," which, as time went on, we eventually sang in both English and French, especially in Quebec, where after much controversy, French became the official language.

The Dominion of Canada was initially formed in 1841 by the union of Upper Canada and Lower Canada. Upper Canada's population consisted largely of former Americans still loyal to Great Britain (that is, English-Canadians living in what is now Ontario), while Lower Canada (today's Quebec) was mainly populated by French-Canadians, with long memories (*je me souviens* is still on Quebec license plates) of defeat to the English on the Plains of Abraham.[58] Thus the tradition of hyphenated Canadians began. As Nova Scotia and New Brunswick joined this Confederation to create the Dominion of Canada in 1867, the Fathers of Confederation agreed that there would be two official languages in this new country, Canada, something that came back to bite Quebec a little more than a century later in the 1970s and 1980s when Separatism reared its controversial head. Suddenly we had a Quebec population divided into Franco-phones, Anglo-phones, and Allo-phones (of neither French- nor English-origin). Separatist or Federalist labels merged into Québécois or ROC (Rest of Canada). And violence.

It seemed to be forgotten that, since Canada's boundaries had grown over time to include ten provinces, plus the Northern Territories, the population now included immigrants from many countries of the world. Over the years, the French/English hyphen had proliferated to include many places of origin. In other words, while the country's inhabitants were and are all "Canadians," at various times in Canadian history, they or their ancestors had migrated from some other land. There were, indeed, many hyphens in Canadian identities. The federal government encouraged Canadians to celebrate the memory of their ethnic or cultural identity as a matter of pride. It added a welcome diversity to society. And eventually, native Canadian "Indians" were dignified with the title "First Nations" people. Canada has long believed that "the cultural mosaic" enriches society. And it certainly has.

Just as it has done in the US, but Americans have traditionally expressed the same idea differently, with belief in "the melting pot"—an "out of many, one" concept: It doesn't matter where you have come from. Once you are a citizen, you are an American, as I am today. And you enrich American culture with your prior knowledge and/or experience of other countries. It's a tradition worth keeping. At the same time, there is a caveat. Don't bring the divisive hatred and hostilities that may have been attached to your old land and bring them to the new one. It is also a place to start anew.

We don't have to wait for Thanksgiving to express deep gratitude for the cultural enrichment immigrants from so many countries have brought and continue to bring over the centuries. It's self-evident. So why do we hold on to the hyphens? Because people are proud of their diverse heritages and consequent self-identification, and, unlike in many other countries, we have the freedom to express that pride. When you have the freedom to travel to so many less developed parts of the world, as I have had the opportunity to do in recent years, you also know how good it is to come home.

The Message of the Waves[59]

*C*ontinually, I try to make space on my bookshelves for new books. That means packing away others because rabbis tend to acquire a lot of books, two large bookcases full, in my case, overflowing on to piles on the floor and in little nooks and crannies around the house. Even my Kindle has grown heavy. I have considered putting the new books in the pantry, but my family dissuaded me. What could I relinquish then? Not books about Jewish history...or thought...or liturgy...or Jewish values. Not Talmudic logic or narrative or Hasidic tales. Certainly not the Torah, the *Tanakh* (entire Hebrew Bible), and all the valuable commentaries I have acquired and continue to acquire over the years. They have become part of me. So I keep taking books off the shelf and putting them back.

One of the books I leafed through was Rabbi Ed Feinstein's *Tough Questions Jews Ask*, a slim little volume intended for young adults.[60] It flew open by itself at a page that addressed the question, "What is God Anyway?" What is the One in the *Shema*? That's what the young adults he teaches want to know. They have been taught to say the *Shema*—six little words, we Jews say them all the time, we cover our eyes to increase concentration. But what does it mean? What does "One" mean?

In reply, the rabbi presented an analogy to the waves in the ocean. Imagine that you are at the ocean, he said, looking at that large body of water. If each wave had awareness, it would understand that it is part of something bigger. Each wave rises and comes to an individual crest—there are small waves and middle-size waves and huge waves (how big will this wave be?)—but their life span is short. They recede and become part of the ocean again. Once more each wave merges to become One.

It is so fascinating, I reflected, that in this century, scientists, great minds like Stephen Hawkings, have been trying to create a "Theory of Everything." There is speculation that if Albert Einstein had lived in the age of Information Technology, he might have developed a formula for "Everything". Now there is an "Internet of Everything." Yet for thousands of years, the "Theory of Everything" has been encoded in six little words in the Torah that end with three words: God is One (*Adonai Echad*).

What Rabbi Feinstein's little book was really teaching these young people about was the ocean of humanity. We are all individual waves that eventually merge with the One, with the Everything. I put the little book back on my shelf. A keeper.

However, the analogy to the ocean didn't mention the destructive power the same waves could unleash if nature ran wild. Or if, as portrayed in the Torah, God decided to destroy mankind by flood for immoral conduct beyond reprieve, a destruction God regretted and promised never to do again.

> "*But My loyalty shall never move from you,*
> *Nor My covenant of friendship be shaken—*
> *said the Lord, who takes you back in love*" (Isaiah 54: 9-10).[61]

This is something to remember as once again our present day world faces threats from multiple sources, including climate change and military action. How do we best use our scientifically awesome individual and collective power? How do we prevent the flood?

I shook off these heavy thoughts and returned to the book shelf. Since one can readily find health care information on the Internet, I removed a large book—a tome, really—dealing with diagnoses and remedies for common medical problems. Then I gasped to see my late mother's handwriting on the book's flyleaf. It looked so much like my own, a little fancier, the letters more open. It was dated 1995 when my mother was 90 and intended as a birthday gift for my daughter.

The inscription explained the etymology of the word *shalom*, one little word this time, one little word that guides our journey on earth from life to death. It is a salutation that greets us when we arrive. "Hello, we are glad you are here." It means not only peace but wholeness, completion. For my mother, *shalom* also meant healing and health, all of which she wished her grand-daughter on her birthday, in effect, the day of my daughter's continued rise to the crest of her individual wave. That is why my mother placed this inscription in a medical book.

Later, my mother explained, not only did *shalom* become *salaam* in Muslim usage, but the Malaysian Muslims adapted it to *salang*. Many years later, British soldiers serving in Southeast Asia during World War II appropriated it when they returned to Britain, and that is how *shalom*, which also means goodbye became the salutation, "So Long."

The salutation grew into an immensely popular song. The lyrics (different versions can be found on the Internet) were first put to music by Woody Guthrie[62] during the depression years in the 1930s, but the song soared to popularity in 1951 when it was recorded by The Weavers,[63] then The Spinners,[64] Pete Seeger,[65] and other musical ensembles. It became a song of my Canadian youth, sung in hale and hearty farewell when people parted:

> *"So long, it's been good to know you …*
> *it's a long time since I've been home."*

This is the message of the waves, I thought. A few little words. Enjoy your brief time as you rise to your towering strength. It's been good to experience the air and the sun and to see far into the land, but don't overpower it. Don't use your strength to destroy. Be the best wave that you can be until it is time to recede into the company of the other waves in the Oneness of your eternal home. It's good to be home. That's what my mother did when she was ninety-three. She went home. To the One, to the "Theory of Everything." Yet her generous spirit still lives in the company of those who knew her, loved her, in the inscribed message of the flyleaf. When we say *shalom* and mean it, we prevent the Flood.

MESSAGE IN A BOTTLE[66]

Tonight,
when distance is an
ocean deep, eons wide,
your call will come
set free...
Enter. I am listening.

Tonight,
when your words crest
waves beyond time
to hand-wash my heart
gently held...
Enter. I am floating.

Tonight,
when eye is to eye,
and soul is to soul...
Save. This sacred moment.

SECTION NINE

Appendix

Jewish Life in Yugoslavia: Treasures of Two Millennia

*M*y involvement with Yugoslavian art—beginning with the Central Museum of Zagreb in Croatia and the Jewish Museum of Belgrade in Serbia—is a story that evolved over a period of years (1984 -1990.) It excited my interest in Yugoslavian art and artists, as well as Jewish history in Yugoslavia (now the former Yugoslavia).[67]

Since I had a considerable professional background in the arts in Canada and long experience as a volunteer in the Jewish community, I was asked to coordinate an international art exhibition, to bring Jewish art treasures from Yugoslavia—it was not yet the former Yugoslavia—to the West. It was then the mid-1980s. The bitter conflict in Yugoslavia had not yet erupted, although it was already feared it was only a matter of time until war would break out.

The Yugoslavian Jewish art treasures have a very different history from the larger, better known Czech collection. The Czech treasures were confiscated from Jewish institutions and people by the Nazis during World War II. They were methodically itemized, tagged, and stored, with the intent to create a museum of an extinct people after the war.

Although the collection of Jewish art treasures from Yugoslavia were similar in nature, ranging from large ceremonial objects to the keys to synagogues in Spain prior to the Inquisition—keys that had been secreted and passed down from generation to generation—these treasures had been hidden from the Nazis by Jewish individuals who buried them and kept them hidden during the subsequent Communist regime as well. They had been buried for fifty years when the emergence of the Czech collection stimulated an interest in gathering treasures

143

from various localities in Yugoslavia to form a Yugoslavian collection. There were many problems involved in doing so, the foremost amongst them legal and diplomatic issues: to whom did the collection belong— the families that had hidden them, the Jews of Yugoslavia, the Jews of the world, the Yugoslav government?

As late as 1984, the Jewish community of Belgrade, terrified that the treasures might be taken from them, was denying to the Chief Sephardic Rabbi, Dr. Salomon Gaon, who visited the community as an emissary to the West, that these treasures even existed. Eventually they were unearthed, gathered together, and sent to Zagreb, the capital of Croatia, for exhibition at the Central Museum. In time, especially as worry about the growing conflict in Bosnia grew, the various Yugoslav groups involved in the exhibit became more amenable to sending "the collection" to the West.

The Sarajevo Haggadah, a beautiful, illuminated, fourteenth century manuscript that had survived both the Spanish inquisition and the Nazis (it was hidden during the Nazi regime behind a brick wall in the home of a Muslim cleric) was the star of the collection. In Toronto, I would meet with Dushka Cohen, whose ancestors originally owned the Sarajevo *Haggadah* and had fled with it to the Balkans at the time of the Spanish Inquisition (the *Haggadah* was so much a part of the family that their children had colored with crayon on some of the pages, and there were some wine stains as well). By 1894, the Cohen family so desperately needed money that they sold the *Haggadah* to the National Museum in Bosnia. Almost a century later, Dushka produced a video telling the story of the Haggadah's journey.

I had already been invited by my longtime friend, the late Honorable Kalman Samuels, a Montreal lawyer who served as Honorary Consul to Yugoslavia, to attend a meeting in New York City. Here I encountered colleagues from both the Central Museum in Zagreb and the Jewish Museum in Belgrade (which was funded from New York), as well as others with whom I had been establishing a relationship since the first organizing meeting with Dr. Salomon Gaon was held at Temple Emmanu-el in Montreal in 1984.

In New York, I stayed at the lovely apartment of Mary Levine, then president of the American Association of Yugoslav Jews, an admirable, elegant woman who for many years had been broadcasting for the *Voice of America* at the United Nations. She was instrumental in smoothing the way for the collection to come to New York and would help bring it to Canada as well. Kalman would facilitate the legal and diplomatic channels to make it possible. Security issues were discussed.

At the meeting, I was formally asked to find a suitable venue in Toronto to mount an exhibition of the treasures there. It would be called "Jewish Life in Yugoslavia: Treasures of Two Millennia." This was no small task, partly because the major museums were aware that a New York exhibition had already been planned at the Jewish Museum in that city; mounts were already made for the exhibition and a catalogue printed, but, at the last minute, the Yugoslav government intervened to cancel the exhibition. The Jewish Museum was left in the lurch. Extensive diplomatic negotiations frantically took place, but after the collection finally arrived in New York, neither the Jewish Museum nor any of the other large museums wanted to touch the exhibition. They were afraid it would be aborted again.

So, with some misgivings, I agreed to give it a try in Toronto. Security concerns were a big consideration for most venues. In Toronto, Canadians of Croatian origin and those of Serbian origin held permitted demonstrations on a main street every weekend. They took turns: one week the Canadian Croats were demonstrating, and the next week it was the turn of Canadians of Serbian origin. On the multicultural radio talk shows, they hurled insults at one another on a daily basis. The museums didn't want trouble. Finally, after my presentations to the Board of Directors of the magnificent *Beth Tzedec* Synagogue, Judith Cardozo, the talented curator of the synagogue's jewel of a museum, agreed to hold the exhibition of "Jewish Treasures from Yugoslavia" there.

It was feasible mainly because this museum already housed the famed, large Cecil Roth collection of Judaica, only part of which could be shown at any one time. Thus if, at the last minute, the Yugoslav exhibit should be cancelled, the museum would still have more than enough to exhibit. The Board stipulated, however, that the exhibit be publicized privately to the membership of synagogues, Jewish schools and institutions, and to invited guests. In most circumstances, it would not be available to the general public. Dr. Salomon Gaon made his own stipulation: the Sarajevo *Haggadah* would not travel from Bosnia to the West for exhibition because he considered the then 600-year old manuscript to be too fragile.

It was a long process. Communications were difficult with Yugoslavia, whether with Zagreb or Belgrade. Fax machines were rare there at that time, and even if computers had been readily available, e-mail did not yet exist. The time difference of six hours meant that I had to make phone contact in the middle of the night, and worry about diplomatic, legal, and security concerns kept me nail-biting (and I am not a nail-biter) until the artifacts finally arrived from New York safe and sound in Toronto. It was now 1990. Six years had passed—we had started the preliminaries of organizing the exhibition in 1984 (when the Jewish community in Belgrade said it didn't exist!).

To say that the exhibition was splendid is an understatement. The staff of the Beth Tzedec's Cecil Roth Museum outdid themselves. The synagogue itself is a magnificent structure, with bronze, sculptured walls and marble floors. Added to this were the exhibit's large and colorful altar mantles (*parochets)* hung not only in the museum and up the lobby's staircase, but also from the high ceilings of the synagogue and the sanctuary. The exhibition continued quietly from October 20 to December 23, 1990, with little publicity outside the Jewish community and many, many attendees. And yes, we used the mounts from the Jewish Museum in New York, as well as the catalogues they had printed. Nothing was wasted.

I was briefly joyful to obtain a grant from the City of Montreal to bring the exhibit to a *Maison de Culture* there, but it was circumvented when hostilities broke out in Yugoslavia. The Jewish Museum in Belgrade nervously requested that the treasures be sent back immediately, not to the Central Museum in Croatia, but to Belgrade. It was my understanding that the treasures could be sent to Israel from Belgrade. Some localities wanted their own artifacts back for another round of safe-keeping. There are many pieces of the puzzle that I don't know and didn't want to know then. What I do know is that all the Jewish art treasures, including the Sarajevo *Haggadah* were safe and in good hands.

However, in 1992, the Sarajevo *Haggadah* was to survive another catastrophe: this time the shelling of the National Museum in Bosnia, where the *Haggadah* was being kept for safety during the raging conflict between Serbs and Croats. The Museum's Muslim director, Enver Imamovic, and three volunteers disregarded their own safety to break into the museum vault and remove the Haggadah. They took it to the National Bank where it was kept in an underground vault throughout the conflict—buried again.

Later, after a visiting delegation from the American Jewish Joint Distribution Committee viewed it, with the help of the United Nations, the Sarajevo *Haggadah* was spirited away to the Austrian Academy of Fine Arts in Vienna for repair by conservator Andrea Pataki, who stabilized the binding but "left the wine stains for history." The fictionalized story of the Sarajevo Haggadah's journey, including its restoration, has been admirably told by Geraldine Brooks in a popular novel called *The People of the Book* (New York: Viking; Penguin Group, 2008).

According to Milica Mihailovic, then curator at the Jewish Historical Museum in Belgrade and the author of *Judaica in Yugoslavia*, "The discovery of the Sarajevo Haggadah had an important impact on the study of Jewish art." ("Introduction," 3).

STUDY GUIDE FOR BOOK GROUPS

Topics to Think About and Discuss: Finding the Balance

Preface: The World We Live In

1. Is perception of personal and social space culturally conditioned?
2. Do we take the concept of upward mobility for granted in developed countries?
3. Have you ever personally experienced a situation where there was no food available for purchase even if you had money?
4. How can our educational system place greater emphasis on learning about other countries, their histories, languages, cultures, and customs?
5. Should travel as a form of education be built into educational systems? How should it be implemented? Should it be subsidized?
6. Immigration issues are a matter of grave concern globally, in the twenty-first century—how can we find a balance between legality, resources, and compassion for those who desperately seek asylum?

Section One: South Pacific, Oceania

1. What would you like to learn about Jewish communities, past and present, around the world?
2. What experience have you had with "Counting the *Omer*" or celebrating with a *Mimouna* at the end of Passover?
3. When is the spirit of the law more important than the letter of the law?

4. In this section, we touched on syncretism (a blending of established religions with expressive native customs). How far can you take it without losing the substance of an established religion?
5. What is the place of ritual in religion?
6. Can you be spiritual without being religious?
7. Can you be religious without being spiritual?
8. Whether you belong to a congregation or *minyan*—or not—what are your concerns about religion today?

Section Two: Australia

1. What does Australia's history teach us about incarceration and prison reform?
2. What do we learn about Australian hospitality? What does the bible teach us about welcoming strangers?
3. How important are food associations (like raisin bread and hot chocolate to the author) in feelings of well-being?
4. In the twenty-first century, do we still need to joke about the need to have three synagogues for two Jews—or do you think greater unity of thought and practice is possible?
5. What do the "little penguins" teach us about the parent-child relationship? About fertility and "divorce"? About the Jewish value of *kehilla*, of community? About appreciating the wonders of the world, however small?

Section Three: Brazil, South America

1. Why does the synagogue in Recife have a sand floor?
2. If you are Jewish, have you ever experienced immersion in a *mikveh*?
3. What part does religion play in saving the Brazilian population from despair? How does religious ritual provide a safety valve for society? Do nativism and established religion support one another?
4. What role does *Carnival* play in Brazilian society?

5. How can a large country with such rich resources have so many people who live in dire poverty? What do we learn about poverty and corruption in Brazil?
6. How is climate change affecting the Amazon? How does the Amazon's rainforest affect the rest of the world?

Section Four: The Mediterranean

1. Where are the Jews? How have the lingering effects of the Spanish Inquisition and later, the Holocaust, affected Jewish populations in Europe and around the world? What effect did the establishment of the State of Israel play?
2. Why do Messianic Jews consider themselves Jewish? Are they?
3. What musical instruments, if any, do you play? Have you ever tried to blow a *shofar*?
4. How do you feel about Interfaith Relations? How can we improve them?
5. How do you feel about interfaith marriages and their impact on the growth or decline of Jewish populations?

Section Five: Panama Canal, Central America

1. In animal life, it usually seems clear which ones are predators, and which are prey. How can you tell whether human beings are predators or prey? Can we be both at different times?
2. In the author's story, a green shoot is the symbol of regeneration—the basis for hope after destruction and an integral part of the history of the Jewish people. Why is it part of human nature to rebuild after disaster? What gives us the strength to do so?
3. How have volcanic eruptions affected this area and its people? What do you think of Antonin Artaud's theories?
4. Why do people continue to live in dangerous areas? How will climate change impact where people live?
5. What have you learned about the Maya and their civilization? In other areas, what remnants of Mayan culture can also be

found (Chichen Itza, Mexico in the Yucatan; Peru)? Have you ever visited any of these sites?

Section Six: Canarias, Spain

1. How do humans and nature interact in these islands?
2. How do art and nature intersect to enhance one another in these locales and elsewhere?
3. In this section, the author describes her spiritual experience in visiting a lava tube in Lanzarote. How can nature's cycles and religious beliefs augment one another?

Section Seven: Southeast Asia

1. Southeast Asia designates a large area, and the author explores the diverse cultures there, some of them very old. Respect for ancestors is a theme throughout. Does that resonate with your values?
2. How have warfare and poverty affected these areas?
3. Why is pollution endangering the environment and way of life of these countries?
4. How is education an issue?
5. Why are natural resources an issue?
6. What drives the governments and people of Singapore, Vietnam, and Hong Kong to be ahead of the curve?
7. What kind of leadership do you think works best in Southeast Asia? It is hard to change old ways. Are new ways always better?

Section Eight: Homecoming

1. Climate change has become an existential issue globally: At *Rosh Hashana*, the Jewish New Year, our most important prayer, *Una Tana Tokef*, asks the same question every year: "Who will live and who will die?..."Who by fire and who by water?" Increasingly, this is a question that concerns us all. Ironically, is this the question that will unite us? Can we prevent "the flood?" Can we make the most of every day we are alive?

2. How do we unify the people and countries of this world in an effort to protect the environment?
3. Human beings are simply people with similar needs, desires, and dreams, wherever they live. Are the major issues that affect humanity held in common everywhere?
4. How do we find the right balance? Can religious practice help?
5. Is it true that there is no place like home?

ACKNOWLEDGMENTS

What I have written in the foregoing sections is the culmination of personal observation and memory of things past and present, information gleaned from the fascinating lectures given by distinguished speakers aboard the various ships on which I traveled, various excellent books, information dispensed on placards and pamphlets in museums, galleries, and historical sites, tourist brochures, and, especially the casual discourse of knowledgeable guides in countries around the world.

In addition, I have occasionally consulted Professor Google for geographic data and the verification of some historical dates and places. The Internet sites, www.myjewishlearning.org, www.jewishvirtuallibrary.org, and Aish.com have been particularly valuable as sources of information throughout and particularly in my section on Southeast Asia.

Thank you to my four daughters, Janet, Shelley, Susan, and Laura, for their helpful critiques and suggestions, and for copy-editing every single page of the manuscript, and especially to Janet for undertaking the formidable job of formatting the footnotes and to Susan for line editing. I am so glad that Janet had the opportunity to go snorkeling in Indonesia, when I couldn't go ashore, to take a small boat through an awe-inspiring dark cavern in the Philippines, and to ride on horseback up the slope of a volcanic mountain. Also that Susan had the chance to snorkel in the waters of Australia's Great Barrier Reef (some of the coral already destroyed by thoughtless tourists).

I would also like to express my heartfelt thanks to my colleague and friend, Rabbi Beth Lieberman, for her editorial comments and publication suggestions. Thank you, too, to Rabbi Belle Michael, Dr. Julie Madorsky, and Chaplain Muriel Dance for taking their precious time to read my book. Much appreciation as well to the production team at Lulu Books Press, Inc. for doing such a good job on my book.

Very special thanks also to Rabbi Edward Feinstein of *Valley Beth Shalom* Synagogue in Los Angeles, where I have spent many meaningful hours, for his inspirational teaching in *Tough Questions Jews Ask: A Young Adult's Guide to Building a Jewish Life*. And to Rabbi David Woznica of Stephen Wise Temple, whom I consulted the traditional three times before I entered rabbinical school, and whose educational programs are always outstanding; to Rabbi Mordecai Finley, who was a major influence on my approach to the divine, and with whom I interned; and to Rabbi Mel Gottlieb, Dean of the Academy of Jewish Religion, California, whose compassion, love, and erudition extend to his students, faculty, and far beyond.

ABOUT RABBI CORINNE COPNICK

MRS (Master of Rabbinic Studies, AJRCA),
MA (Developmental Drama, McGill),
BA (Honors English, McGill), CM (Canada Medal)

What an incredible journey! Born in Montreal, Quebec, Canada, Rabbi Corinne Copnick moved to Los Angeles, California in 2000 to be near her children and rapidly emerging grandchildren. She is the proud mother of four wonderful daughters and three amazing grandchildren, two already in college. Also the grandmother of three dogs.

With a rich background in the multidisciplinary arts (including as a CBC national radio actress in her youth, an art gallery owner in mid-life, and a writer throughout), Rabbi Corinne—as she prefers to be called—was ordained as a rabbi and teacher in 2015 at the age of seventy-nine. Currently she serves as a *dayan* (judge in a rabbinic court) and Governor of the Sandra Caplan Community Bet Din (SCCBD) in Los Angeles. She also founded and teaches a pluralistic study group, *Beit Kulam* (House of Togetherness), now in its sixth year. As a rabbinic resource, she applies artistic modalities to education about contemporary Jewish living.

Since ordination, she has been serving as a Guest Staff Rabbi on lengthy cruises to Hawaii and other islands in the Caribbean, the ABC islands, the South Pacific Islands, Australia, the Panama Canal, Central and South America, Mexico, the Mediterranean, and Southeast Asia. Ergo—the genesis of *A Rabbi at Sea: A Unique Spiritual Journey.*

Rabbi Corinne is the author of several published books: *Embrace: A Love Story in Poetry* (bilingual poems in English and French); *Altar Pieces*, narrated and screened for five years on Canada's Vision TV, and

157

for which she was honored with the Canadian Commemorative Medal (1992), awarded to those who have made a significant contribution to Canada; *How To Live Alone Until You Like It—And Then You Are Ready For Somebody Else*; and *Cryo Kid: Drawing a New Map*, awarded finalist status in the 2009 National Indie Awards of Excellence. For several years, she was Entertainment Editor for *Jewish Life* and a regular columnist for *The Jewish Tribune* in Toronto. The recipient of various grants and scholarships, she was honored to serve as resident writer at the Banff Center for the Arts, Alberta. Simultaneously, for fifteen years, she ran a successful writing and editing business.

In her prior Montreal life, as owner of *Galerie La Magie de l'Art*, Rabbi Corinne created more than forty stellar exhibitions and cultural events. She designed a groundbreaking role-playing simulation on Canadian unity called "Future Directions." An acclaimed play that she wrote for drug education purposes, *Metamorphose*, was featured at the Quebec Pavilion of Montreal's *Man and His World*, as well as many other venues. In 1991, in cooperation with the Central Museum of Zagreb and the Jewish Museum in Belgrade, she organized an outstanding international exhibition, held in Toronto, of "Jewish Art Treasures from the former Yugoslavia."

In addition, she has always been active as a volunteer. In 1998, the National Council of Jewish Women (Montreal section) honored her, with other past presidents, as a Woman of Distinction. She served in an executive volunteer role on the Boards of The Quebec Drama Festival, the St. James Literary Society, National Council of Jewish Women, and Temple Emmanu-el Beth Shalom. In Toronto, she was on the Boards of Medina Theatre and the Jewish Theatre Committee of Greater Toronto. In California, she served for several years on the Boards of West Coast Jewish Theatre and the Canadian Women's Club of Los Angeles.

NOTES

1 A contemporary interpretation by the author, ©Corinne Copnick, Los Angeles, 2019, of the traditional Traveler's Prayer, *Tefilat Haderech*.

2 Lyrics adapted from "Traveling Towards a Dream," ©Corinne Copnick, Toronto, 1994; Los Angeles, 2019. Musical arrangements by ©Nathan Rosen ("Traveling Towards A Dream"), Toronto, 1994, and ©Ira Brown ("Some Dream"), BMI, 04/14/1994).

Section 2: Australia

3 Natalie Rosinsky, "Esther Abrahams: From Convict to 'First Lady,' " www. natalierosinsky.com/2014/07/12/esther-abraham-from-convict-to-first-lady, July 12, 2014. Posted as an article on the *Gone Graphic* blog under the archive "Jews."

4 Rosinsky, "Esther Abrahams: From Convict to First Lady."

5 Much of the following information was gleaned from a comprehensive lecture, including some printed material, at the old synagogue, which is still in use. For those who are interested in additional historical detail about the Great Synagogue's history, an excellent book by the Rabbi Emeritus, Rabbi Dr. Raymond Apple, is available: *The Great Synagogue: A History of Sydney's Big Shule*, UNSW PRESS, 2008.

6 Apple, *The Great Synagogue.*

7 Apple, *The Great Synagogue.*

8 Apple, *The Great Synagogue.*

9 Apple, *The Great Synagogue.*

10 Apple, *The Great Synagogue.*

Section 3: Brazil, South America

11 In Recife the name is pronounced as Hecife. The "R" at a beginning of a word is pronounced as an "H." When you get to Rio de Janeiro, Recife is pronounced the way it is spelled, with an "R" sound.

12 See https://www.jewishvirtuallibrary.org/brazil-virtual-jewish-history-tour and multiple other sites on the Internet.

13 Matthew Wells, "10 Terrifying Creatures of the Amazon," https://Listverse.com, Sept. 27, 2013.

14 Wells, "Ten Terrifying Creatures of the Amazon."

15 I verified these figures on Google.com.

16 I verified President Carmona's biography on Google.com also.

Section 4: Panama Canal, Central America, South America

17 Throughout this section concerning the Maya, I have referred to the writings of Michael Coe as an authority. Michael Coe, *Breaking the Maya Code*, 3rd ed. (USA: Thames and Hudson; Amazon Books, 2011), chap.2, Kindle, 2019.

18 *The Zohar*, Pritzker Edition, Trans. and Commentary by Daniel C. Matt, Stanford, California: Stanford University Press, 2004 (Zohar Education Project); Arthur Green, *A Guide to the Zohar*, Stanford, California: Stanford University Press, 2004. The Zohar is a mythical commentary on the Torah.

19 The *Book of Enoch* does not appear in the Hebrew Bible; rather, it is an ancient Hebrew apocalyptic text ascribed to Enoch.

20 Enoch is believed to have been the great-grandfather of Noah.

21 Michael Coe, *Breaking the Maya Code*, 3rd ed., Kindle, 2019, location 1108, 1113.

22 In addition, a system of bars and dots are accurately used to represent the numbers (e.g., a dot stands for one, and a bar for five, so that the number six would be a bar and a dot). Coe, *Breaking the Maya Code* (chap.2, Kindle; location 1121).

23 Coe, *Breaking the Maya Code* (chap. 2, Kindle, location 1121).

24 In 2019 CE (the solar calendar in general use), the ancient Hebrew lunar calendar marked the year 5779—until the Jewish New Year (*Rosh Hashana*) in late September, when it became the Hebrew calendar year 5780. It will remain so through 2020 CE until the next *Rosh Hashana*, when it will become Hebrew calendar year 5781 in August. And so on.

25 *JPS Hebrew-English Tanakh: The Traditional Hebrew Text And The New JPS Translation*, 2nd ed. (Philadelphia: The Jewish Publication Society, 1999 -5759), 870.

26 Considerable information about Equine Therapy can be found in "The Efficacy of Equine Assisted Therapy," https://pdfs. semanticscholar.org.

27 Albert Bermel, *Artaud's Theatre of Cruelty* (UK: Bloomsbury Academic, 2008).

Section 5: The Mediterranean

28 The full Edict can be read online at www.sephardicstudies.org and other sites. Also, an interesting article by Miriam Annenberg appeared on the BBC news internet site, https://www.bbcnews/stories-49374489, August 18, 2019. Annenberg's story details the revival in recent years of a small Jewish community on the island of Majorca, which is part of Spain. Surprisingly, this revival was aided by *Chuetas* (the word for *Conversos* in Catalan), whose ancestors had been forced to convert to Christianity hundreds of years ago.

29 It reflected my own feelings as, once again, a guest rabbi on a cruise ship, this time to the Mediterranean.

30 www.jewishvirtuallibrary.org, accessed 2019.

31 https://en.wikipedia.org, accessed 2019.

32 One of our guides through the Jewish quarter insisted that the Spanish Inquisition had nothing to do with the Catholic Church.

33 Daniella Levy, "Dear Spain: Want to Attract Jews? You're Doing It Wrong," *Scribe:* The Forward's Contributor Network, *Forward*, July 24, 2017, https://forward.com/scribe/377722/dear-spain-want-to-attract-jews-youre-doing-it-wrong, accessed 2019.

34 Chabad is an acronym. See p. 132 to find out what the acronym means.

35 *Machzor for the Days of Awe: A High Holy Day Prayer Book,* revised edition. Los Angeles: Stephen S. Wise Temple, 1991) 39-40, 138.

36 Milica Mihailovic, *Judaica in Yugoslavia*, English trans. Bosko Colak-Antic. (Belgrade; Zagreb: Decje Novine, Gornji Milanovac, Thomira Matijevica, Proex Posveta, 1990), "Introduction," 3-4.

37 Mihailovic, *Judaica in Yugoslavia*, English trans. Bosko Colak-Antic, "Introduction," 3.

38 Mihailovic, *Judaica in Yugoslavia*, English trans. Bosko Colak-Antic, "Introduction," 3.

39 Barbados is one of my favorite Caribbean islands. Over the years, I had been there several times. The most memorable of these visits—up to this one, that is—had been forty years earlier at the time of the gifting of the old Jewish synagogue, *Nidhe Israel*, built in Bridgetown in 1654, to the city government.

Synagogue membership had fallen away in recent years; indeed, there were only some forty or so Jews at the time living on the island by the time Barbados became independent in 1983. The synagogue was then seized by the government and scheduled for demolition. The small Jewish community, however, reclaimed it and thus saved it from destruction. Instead, they gifted it to the city of Bridgetown, with the intention that the synagogue would be restored as a Jewish museum for all time.

Since an independent Barbados still had Commonwealth ties to Great Britain, that little community of forty Jews worked non-stop to make it happen. With great determination, they called on Jewish leaders from all over the Commonwealth to assist in the synagogue's renewal as a museum celebrating the history of Jewish life in Barbados. And assist they did. Active members of synagogues and/or other Jewish institutions all over the Commonwealth came to Barbados. The necessary money was raised, and a gala dinner for all the Commonwealth guests, as well as government officials, was held on site. The government of Barbados even issued a special stamp to commemorate the occasion!

There were other surrounding events as well to welcome the Commonwealth guests, and, because I was a close friend of one of the delegates from Canada (and active in the Jewish community as well), I was invited to several of them.

By an amazing coincidence, when my daughter Janet and I arrived in Barbados, it was the fortieth anniversary of the dedication of the old synagogue as a museum. This knowledge imparted a special flavor to our visit. The museum and adjacent gem of a small synagogue (it looked like a miniature of the much larger synagogue I had visited in Recife, Brazil) had both been beautifully conceived and restored. We felt very proud to be there.

It even had a *mikveh*, but since the *mikveh* was partially surrounded by stone walls, it was categorized by the Barbadian government as an *indoor* pool, which, according to Barbados law, therefore had to be chlorinated. In Jewish law, however, a *mikveh* cannot be chlorinated; the water must be pure. So the *mikveh* could not be used. It was very pretty, though. "Don't touch the water!" we were warned.

40 Rabbi Abraham Joshua Heschel is the author of many books published by Farrar, Strauss and Giroux, New York and considered classics today. Among them, I particularly treasure *The Sabbath* (New York, 1951; paperback, 2015); *God in Search of Man*; *Man is Not Alone: A Philosophy of Religion* (New York,1951); and *Moral Grandeur and Spiritual Audacity: Essays* (New York, 1997), with an introduction by his daughter, Susannah Heschel. Paperback and Kindle editions exist today as well.

41 Bob Oré Abitbol, *Le Gout des Confitures*, French edition,(Montreal: Hurtubise HMH/L'arbre, 1986).

Section 7: Southeast Asia

42 I am grateful to the invaluable Internet sites, www.myjewishlearning.org; www.jewishvirtuallibrary.org ; and Aish.com, especially the insightful "Visual History Tours" on their sites, for much of this background information on Southeast Asia.

Singapore:

43 It is very helpful to consult the following excellent sites for more detailed information on Singapore:

- www.jewishvirtuallibrary.org, accessed 2019.
- The Jewish Community of Singapore/*Beit Hatfutsot*; "Singapore, a tiny heaven for Jews," *Ynet News*, www.ynetnews.com, accessed 2019.
- "Singapore: Culture and Community"/Reform Judaism.org, https://reformjudaism.org, accessed 2019.
- "Singapore Jew: Synagogue Singapore/*Maghain-Arboth*," https://www.singaporejews.com, accessed 2019.
- Crazy Rich Asian Jews—Singapore's least known elite," www.haaretz.com, accessed 2019.
- "Community in Singapore." World Jewish Congress, www.worldjewishcongress.org, accessed 2019.

Thailand:

44 Since I could not disembark, I found the following sites most informative, especially in terms of historical verification and dates:

- www.jewishvirtuallibrary.org, accessed 2019.
- Community in Thailand—World Jewish Congress, www.worldjewishcongress.org, accessed 2019.
- "The Jews in Thailand," https://dbs.bh.org, accessed 2019.
- "History of the Jews in Thailand," https://en.wikipedia.org, accessed 2019.
- "The Jewish Community of Thailand," www.jewishthailand.com, accessed 2019.

Cambodia:

45 See Christopher Hudson, *The Killing Fields* (based on "The Death and Life of Dith Pran," an article by journalist Sydney Schanberg), Pan Books, 1984, as well as a 1984 British biographical drama, also titled *The Killing Fields* by Goldcrest Films (DVD version starring Sam Waterston) about the *Khmer Rouge* regime, are both available on Amazon.com.

    Useful information about the atrocities committed by the *Khmer Rouge* is also provided by *Survival After the Killing Fields* by Haing Ngor, with contributions by Roger Warner (NY Carroll and Graf Publishers, 2003). Haing Ngor was a medical doctor.

46 See also Pulitzer Prize-winning Elizabeth Becker's heart-rending book, *When the War Was Over: Cambodia and the Khmer Rouge Revolution* (1st Public Affairs ed., 1998; Kindle, accessed 2019). Becker covered Cambodia during the Revolution for the *Washington Post*, and she also wrote for the *New York Times*. *When the War was Over* won a Robert F. Kennedy book award.

Vietnam:

47 "History of the Jews in Vietnam," https://en.wikipedia.org, accessed 2019. Jews are a minor ethno-religious group of Vietnam, presently consisting of about 300 people.

48 "Vietnamese Jew—Chabad," https://www.chabad.org, August 30, 2009, accessed 2019.

Darwin:

49 "Darwin, Northern Territory," https// https://en.wikipedia.org/wiki/Darwin,_Northern_Territory, accessed 2019.

50 "Art Gallery of the Northern Territory," https://en.wikipedia.org/wiki/Museum_and_Art_Gallery_of_the_Northern_Territory, accessed 2019.

Indonesia:

51 Additional background on Indonesia can be found on this sites.

- "History of the Jews in Indonesia," https://en.wikipedia.org, March 2019, accessed 2019.
- "The Jews in Indonesia/Facts, stories, and anecdotes", www.dbs.bh.org, accessed 2019.

- "Inside the secret world of Indonesia's Jewish community", www.haaretz. com, accessed 2019.
- "Indonesia's Jews: Small Jewish community faces growing intolerance," *DW News*, https:// www.dw.com; YouTube, accessed 2019.
- "Jews live in the shadows in Muslim majority Indonesia," March 3, 2019, *https://www.nst.com.my/world/2019/03/466095/jews-live-shadows-musli m-majority-indonesia*, accessed 2019.
- "The Synagogue of Surabaya, Indonesia"/*Beit Hafutsot*, www.bh.org, accessed 2019.

52 See Yula Egorova, *Jews and Muslims in South Asia: Reflections on Difference, Race, and Religion* (UK:Oxford University Press, 2018). Her book explores the history of Judaism and Islam in South Asia, with emphasis on India. It examines how Jewish and Muslim communities interact in ways that don't fit Western stereotypes.

Philippines:

53 Carl Hoffman, "The Philippines: A Distant Haven From The Holocaust," *The Jerusalem Post*, April 25, 2017.
54 Noel M. Izon, *An Open Door: Jewish Rescue in the Philippines*. Documentary film, www.imdb.com. Extended trailer uploaded to Netflix, https://youtube, and Aish.com, accessed 2019.
55 Frank Ephraim. *Escape to Manila: From Nazi Tyranny to Japanese Terror*, (US: University of Illinois Press, 2008).
    See also Jonathan Goldstein. *Jewish Identities in East and Southeast Asia: New Perspectives on Modern Jewish History, vol 6*, ed. Cornelia Wilhelm (Germany: De Gruyter Oldenbourg, 2015).
56 "Duterte: I will not allow my country to be destroyed by drugs,"...https:// www.asianjournal.com>Philippines>across-the-islands>Duterte-ii-, Feb. 22, 2019

Hong Kong:

57 Hong Kong was formerly a British colony. However, while Hong Kong is now formally a part of China, they still have different systems of government. Generally speaking, Jews have not been involved in the massive protests against projected changes in the law that occured a few months after our visit to Hong Kong, mostly because most Jews are expatriates living in Hong Kong mainly for business interests. See Jewish Telegraphic Agency's article, "Why

165

most Jews in Hong Kong Are Not Involved in the Protests?" www.jta.org, accessed 2019.

Section Eight: Homecoming

58 "Discover Canada: The Story of Us," television documentary series produced by CBC with the participation of The Bell Fund, www.cbc.ca, 2017, accessed 2019.

59 Excerpted from Corinne Copnick, *Cryo Kid: Drawing a New Map*, (iuniverse, 2008), 157-159.

60 Rabbi Edward Feinstein, *Tough Questions Jews Ask: A Young Adult's Guide to Building a Jewish Life*, 1st ed., 2003, 2nd ed. 2012 (Woodstock, VT: Jewish Lights Publishing).

61 *JPS Hebrew-English Tanakh: The Traditional Hebrew Text And The New JPS Translation*, 2nd ed., 973.

62 ©1949 (renewed 1950, 1951). Woody Guthrie Publications, Inc., ©TRO-Ludlow Music, Inc. (BMI). First released in 1935, and part of his album, Dust Bowl Ballads. World War II version can be found on Internet, https://www.woodyguthrie.org. Lyrics>So-Long-Its-Been-Good-WWII.

63 Modified Lyrics©T.R.O. Inc. Lyrics Licensed and Provided by Lyrics Find. "So Long (It's Been Good to Know You." STANDS4LLC, 2019. Web//Nov. 2019, https://www.lyrics.com/lyric/17353638/ The Weavers>. The Weavers sang traditional folk songs from around the world in the 1950s and 60s.

64 The Spinners, https://www.youtube.com, accessed 2019.

65 Pete Seeger, https://www.youtube.com, June 14, 2014, accessed 2019.

66 Adapted from *Altar Pieces*, Collection of Poems and Stories by ©Corinne Copnick, film adaptation screened on Vision TV, a Canadian National Network, 1992-97.